SCRAP QUILTS

FROM CRUMBS, STRIPS & STRINGS

Use up every last piece with 15 scrap quilt patterns

EMILY BAILEY

DAVID & CHARLES
PUBLISHING

www.davidandcharles.com

CONTENTS

INTRODUCTION

Quilters have always been thrifty, resourceful and endlessly creative. These are traits that are as vital today as they were in the past. In the world of scrap quilting, the humble fabric strip or leftover crumb – those little bits often discarded – become an opportunity for something beautiful. The art of working with fabric strips and crumbs celebrates the chance to transform these small remnants into stunning quilts that are both artistic and practical.

Much like their predecessors, modern quilters know the value of every crumb of fabric. What might seem like a leftover from yesterday's project is actually a rich source of new possibilities. By embracing these smaller pieces, quilters can stretch their fabric budget while creating quilts that reflect personal style and ingenuity. The beauty of working with fabric strips and crumbs lies in the creative freedom it offers, allowing quilters to mix and match textures, colours and patterns from past projects into something entirely new.

Drawing from the rich traditions of quilting history, this method brings the art of using fabric scraps into the present, with contemporary techniques and fresh ideas. In this book, each and every quilt made from strips and crumbs tells a story, filled with memories of past projects, favourite fabrics and the hands that crafted them. From traditional designs to innovative new patterns, the designs are a remix of old and new, creating timeless treasures that are as beautiful as they are resourceful.

Whether you're a seasoned quilter or a beginner, embracing the art of scrappy fabric strips and crumbs offers a satisfying way to create unique, one-of-a-kind quilts. The process invites quilters to explore new ways to use every inch of fabric, turning leftovers into works of art that bring warmth, beauty and joy into your home.

KISS: Keep an eye out for the 'keep it simple sewist' (KISS) tips sprinkled throughout this book. These little gems are here to simplify your scrap-quilting journey. From clever cutting shortcuts to stress-free sewing techniques, KISS tips are your go-to for making quilting as easy and enjoyable as possible. Who needs extra stress? Whether you're a beginner or a seasoned quilter, these bite-sized tips are designed to save time, reduce fuss and help you focus on the fun of turning scraps and strips into stunning quilts.

TOOLS & MATERIALS

Cutting tools

A lot of your success in quilt-making will come from precision in cutting. Having the right tools makes accuracy much easier.

Cutting mats

I like to use a 24 x 36in self-healing cutting mat for cutting out my background and crumb-fabric pieces. I prefer a 12in square self-healing cutting mat when making crumb fabric, as the smaller size means I can keep the mat next to my sewing machine so I can trim off uneven edges as I go.

Quilting rulers

Gridded acrylic rulers for quilting come in many sizes. Use a 6 x 24in ruler for cutting pieces for your quilts. When making crumb fabric I like to use a smaller ruler – a 4 x 8in ruler is my favourite as it is small enough to use next to my sewing machine but long enough to allow me to make a good-sized chunk of crumb fabric.

I have found that a flying geese ruler really cuts down on waste when cutting up my crumb fabric. Squares, half-square triangles and quarter-square triangles can all be cut from a strip of fabric. Cutting instructions for using a flying geese ruler are given in Creating the Basics, Cutting.

Rotary cutters

Choose a rotary cutter that fits comfortably in your hand. Using a sharp blade will save time, making cutting easier and more accurate (uncut threads or untrimmed sections can cause crumb fabric to distort your work). If you need to go over the fabric more than once to cut it, it's time for a new blade. Trust me, taking time to replace a blade is well worth it.

Scissors

It is useful to keep a small pair of scissors or snippers near your sewing machine for cutting threads and tidying up bulk around the edges of your crumb fabric as you make it. A seam ripper is also handy, as when things don't go together as planned a little unpicking may be in order.

AccuQuilt Fabric Cutter

The AccuQuilt cutting machine is a quilter's best friend. Say goodbye to endless cutting and hello to more sewing fun. It slices through multiple fabric layers with perfect precision, saving time and keeping your quilt blocks spot-on. Plus, it's super easy on your hands and back – my wrist no longer aches after cutting out. I love mine!

Sewing tools

The right tools make things easier and help with accuracy. The following will help you be successful in creating your quilts.

Sewing machine

Your sewing machine does not need to be fancy. As long as you can sew a straight ¼in seam then you are good to go. Zigzag and other decorative stitches are a bonus, but not necessary. If you wish to free-motion quilt, you will need a machine that allows you to drop the feed dogs.

Presser feet

I recommend using a ¼in presser foot to help with accuracy when piecing. But a strip of masking (painter's) tape lined up ¼in from your needle will also work. I like to use an open presser foot when doing appliqué as it gives me a better view of where I'm stitching as I sew around motifs. A walking foot is necessary for straight-line quilting and a darning foot is required for free-motion quilting. Personally, as I like my quilting to be more organic, I don't use a walking foot, finding a darning foot to be sufficient.

Machine needles

Universal needles in size 80/12 or size 75/11 work well for piecing and quilting. With sewing machine needles, the larger the number the thicker the shaft. If you are experiencing broken needles, try using a larger needle. It's a good idea to change your needle after 6–8 hours of sewing as they do get blunt, and change immediately if you nick a pin, or your needle bends or breaks. Skipped stitches and puckering can occur when your needle is dull, bent or the wrong size.

Pins and clips

Long straight pins, with a ball or flat head, that are sharp and designed for quilting are useful when matching up seams and points. As well as evenly applying borders and longer sections in your quilts, dividing up long seams and pinning them will help to eliminate wavy, ruffling edges.

Safety pins are my favourite tool for basting quilt layers together. Use the large curved pins designed for quilting, not standard safety pins. The curve makes it easier to get the pin down through the quilt layers and then back up to the quilt front. You will need at least one hundred pins to baste a quilt.

Binding clips are perfect for holding your binding in place while sewing it on. A less expensive option is children's hairclips, which you can often find in discount stores. You can also buy quilters' clips in a range of sizes – the smaller ones can be used in place of pins for some jobs.

Pressing

A standard iron and ironing board are ideal for quilt-making. When making crumb fabric, use steam and spray starch to get a clean finish and make cutting later easier. Remember to press and not iron. Pressing is putting the iron down and holding it. Ironing is moving the iron around, which can distort your fabric.

Marking tools

From time to time you will need to mark on your quilt tops, such as marking a quilting pattern. Water-soluble markers are a good choice, as is tailor's chalk. Choose what will show up best on your fabric and will be easy to remove later. I sometimes use a Hera marker – a plastic tool that creates sharp light creases – which I find particularly useful for marking out straight guidelines for quilting.

Design wall

A design wall is a great asset when it comes to arranging your crumb quilts. Essentially, it is a giant flannel board where you can lay out your quilt. Quilt blocks and fabric pieces stick to it without pins, allowing you to step back and get the big picture on how your colour and design elements are coming together, so you can get a feel for what your quilt will look like before sewing it together. While it doesn't always eliminate 'kissing cousins' (two of the same fabric touching), it does helps. You can use a flannel-backed tablecloth pinned to the wall or make your own 'wall' from foam-core board and flannel.

Appliqué tools

The right tools will help you to achieve perfect appliqué motifs.

Lightweight fusible interfacing'

Lightweight fusible interfacing allows you to get a nice finished edge on your fabric appliqué motifs. By stitching around your appliqué piece with the fusible side next to the fabric and then slitting in the centre and turning the shape through, once turned, you can fuse the motif to your background fabric. Adding a decorative stitch around the raw edges will gives the motif more durability. (See Creating the Basics, Machine appliqué.)

Handy extras

A Purple Thang (a plastic tool), a craft stick and/or a capped pen are useful for running around the edges of your appliqué motifs when they have been turned through, as doing this helps to give the shape a crisp edge and defined points. A glue stick is great for holding motifs in place before securing by sewing.

Fabrics, threads and wadding (batting)

Using high-quality products will give your finished quilt a beautiful look and ensure that it lasts.

NOTE **The projects in this book assume a minimum usable width of fabric of 42in (107cm).**

Background and backing fabrics

These should be good-quality quilting cottons. You can use solids or mix it up by using an assortment of different colours and prints for your backgrounds. While white/ cream is clean and easy to match with your made crumb fabrics, using a coloured background can add something unexpected to your quilt. Another way to do this is to use a small-scale print, low-volume or tone-on-tone background fabrics.

For backing fabrics, good-quality quilting cottons are also ideal. Some fabric ranges come in extra-wide widths especially for backings, which may save you having to join pieces. Or you may wish to carry the scrappy theme to the back of your quilt and use larger leftovers to create a backing fabric of the required size.

Scrap and crumb fabrics

These too should be good-quality quilting cottons. Though, sometimes I throw linens and cotton lawns (finer cottons) into my made crumb fabrics, so do experiment. Scraps should be at least 1in in any one direction, but no bigger than 5in, unless it's a skinny strip when 8–10in long is fine. Using a variety of colours will give your made crumb fabric greater interest. You may wish to use all bright fabrics or all muted fabrics in a made crumb-fabric piece, or you could mix them. If you like the effect you are creating, go for it – there are no rules, only guidelines. When creating made crumb fabric in a single colourway make sure you include a wide range of values (i.e. light and dark shades) to add interest.

When making crumb fabric, baskets or tubs are useful for sorting and holding your scraps while you work, as it keeps them contained but allows you to easily find that next perfect piece.

Threads

High-quality 50-weight cotton thread in a neutral colour is best for creating your crumb fabric. When piecing, you can match the thread with your background fabric/s or continue with neutral thread.

Wadding (batting)

This is the middle layer of your quilt that goes between the quilt top and the backing fabric. Waddings are made from different materials, such as polyester, cotton, cotton-poly blends, wool, silk and bamboo. Cotton wadding will shrink slightly when washed, so, if you don't pre-wash it, it will give your quilt a crinkly softness when the quilt is laundered. I generally use a low-loft cotton-poly blend wadding as it is easy for me to machine quilt. Loft is the thickness of the wadding – the lower the loft, the thinner the wadding. Try out different waddings to find which works best for you.

CREATING THE BASICS

Discover the joy of scrap quilting with strips and crumbs. It's earth friendly and creatively stimulating. Sewing tiny scraps into crumb fabric or strips into sets gives you a colourful way to spice up your quilt projects.

MAKING CRUMB FABRIC

1 Find two similar-sized scraps. If they don't have a straight edge, cut one. Place the scraps right sides together and sew along straight edge. Open out and press.

2 Straighten up edges as needed.

3 For odd-shaped pieces, line up straight edges on the lines on your mat so the pieces create a 90-degree angle and angled pieces overlap slightly.

4 Cut through the overlapped pieces so the angles match.

KISS: Making sure angles match creates crumb fabric that will lay flat. Don't worry about having lots of angles and weird shapes as they will occur naturally as you cut your crumb fabric.

5 I like to place triangular-shaped scraps in a pile. When I find two of a similar size, angle and shape, I sew them together.

6 Chain four or five of these units through your machine (see General Techniques, Piecing).

7 Press your two piece unit then find a scrap that will fit along one edge. Place right sides together and sew to join.

8 Straighten up edges as needed. ▶

9 Continue to add scraps around the edge of the forming crumb fabric in a rail fence or Log Cabin fashion.

10 As pieces get bigger, join two similar-sized pieces.

11 Continue this process until the crumb fabric reaches the desired size. Before cutting, spray with starch to make it more stable.

MAKING CRUMB-FABRIC BACKGROUNDS

1 For pieces smaller than 3in square, use scraps rather than crumb fabric. Using lots of different fabrics will give the crumb-fabric effect without having to deal with lots of seams.

2 When making crumb fabric for larger background pieces, feel free to use larger scraps. It will look great to have small pieces thrown in, but it will take a lot of time to make all of the background with tiny pieces.

3 Use spray starch to stabilise larger pieces before cutting into the desired background pieces. Avoid bulky seams near edges. If your cut is within ¼in of a seam unpick or cut away excess layers of fabric

KISS: Keeping your background fabrics to a colour family and of the same value will prevent the background from taking over your design.

MAKING A STRIP/STRING SET

1 Place two strips right sides together. Press to set a ¼in seam and then join along one long edge.

2 Continue adding strips and strings in the same way until you get to the desired width.

3 Subcut segments of the required width (details are in the project instructions).

4 When a string or strip in your set becomes too short to cut the required segment width, cut the strip set at that point.

5 Alternatively, unpick the short strip and toss it into your crumb bin.

6 Continue adding longer strips to create more strip sets.

KISS: Varying the length of the strips added to the strip set so it 'runs out' (see Steps 5 and 6) enables you to create variety without having to make a lot of different strip sets.

KISS: As well as strips, you can use strings to make strip sets – strings are simply longer scraps and are a super-efficient use of leftovers! I often use strings in smaller strip sets, which is a great way to add more variety. If you wish, you can trim a string so it is the same width across its length, or you can leave the strings as they are to create wonkier-looking strip sets. When using uneven-width strings it can be difficult to get your strip set to lay flat, so it is best to sew them onto a foundation.

MACHINE APPLIQUÉ

Appliqué

1 Trace your shape onto the non-fusible side of lightweight fusible interfacing.

2 Cut the shape out roughly, leaving at least ½in all around it.

3 Place the fusible side of the interfacing against the right side of your desired appliqué fabric.

4 Stitch on the drawn line of your shape.

5 Cut out ¼in beyond the stitched line. If there are tips, clip them, taking care not to snip into your stitching.

6 Pull the interfacing away from the appliqué fabric, then make a slit in the interfacing only.

7 Turn the shape right side out through the slit.

8 Use a Purple Thang (see Tools & Materials) or a capped pen to push out the points, and also to run along the seams to make a crisp edge. Alternatively, a wallpaper roller can be used to give a crisp edge.

9 Position the appliqué shape in the desired spot. Press in place and then topstitch or blanket stitch around the outer edge to secure.

KISS: If using crumb fabric, feel around the edge of your interfacing shape to ensure you don't have bulky seams. Adjust the position of the shape as needed to avoid this.

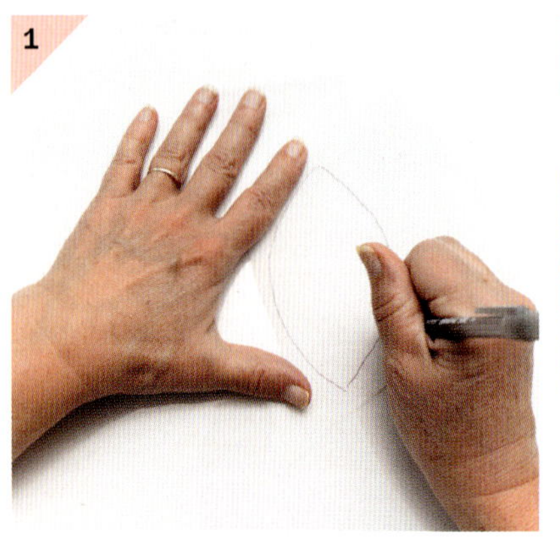

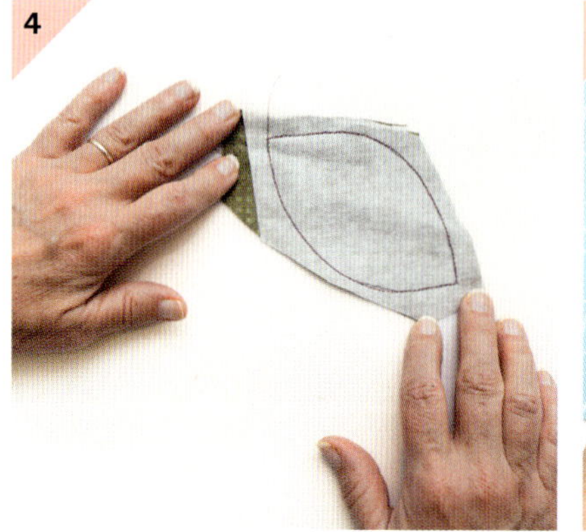

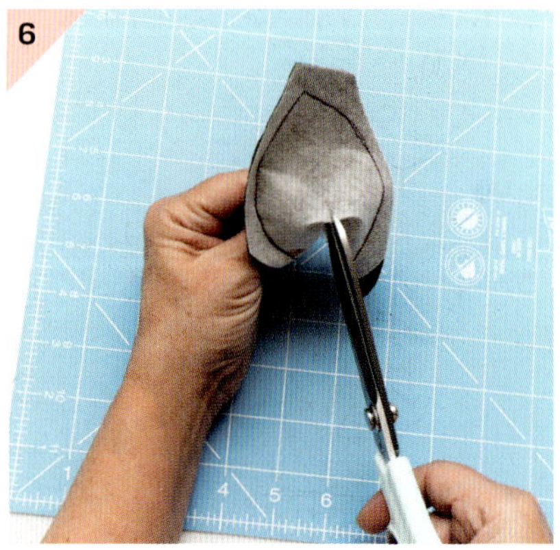

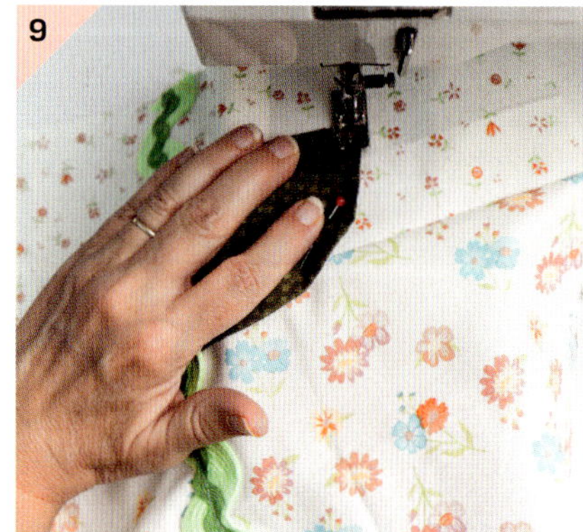

Circle preparation

1 Trace the circle template onto the wrong side of the desired fabric.

KISS: An old cereal box is great for making circle templates.

KISS: You can choose a solid fabric or crumb fabric, or, as here, a four-patch with the circle centred in the unit.

2 Sew a line of basting stitches ¼in beyond the drawn line. Cut the circle out ¼in beyond the line of basting stitches.

3 Begin to pull the basting thread tails until the circle begins to close in on itself.

4 Insert the cardboard circle template into the circle, matching up the template with the drawn line.

5 Continue to pull the basting thread tails until the template is firmly enclosed in the circle. Make sure the edges are flat and even.

6 Press with steam and/or starch to crisp the edge.

7 Pop out the cardboard and appliqué in place as for other appliquéd shapes.

KISS: Pressing the circle after the template has been removed will further crisp the edge for a nice finish.

CUTTING

When cutting appliqué pieces, a sharp pair of scissors is best. However, rotary cutters are useful for getting an accurate straight line when cutting pieces of fabric. In some projects, I used an AccuQuilt Fabric Cutter (an AccuQuilt logo is next to the Cutting instructions where this applies), which offers a quick and easy alternative to rotary cutting.

SAFETY: Rotary cutters are very sharp. When not in use make sure the blade is covered. When cutting, make sure fingers are away from the blade. With the hand that holds the cutter, keep fingers on the handle away from the blade. With the hand not holding the cutter, keep fingers firmly on the cutting ruler, away from the ruler's edges.

Squaring-up your fabric

1 Press the fabric to get rid of any wrinkles.

2 Fold the fabric in half across its width, i.e. so selvedge edges meet. Ensure there are no wrinkles – your cut edges may not line up.

3 Place a 6 x 24in ruler on the fabric so that the 1in line is on the fold and the 24in edge of the ruler runs along one of the cut edges of the fabric, making sure that the ruler is over a double thickness of fabric.

4 Cut along the edge of the ruler nearest to the cut edges to straighten up the edge.

Cutting crumb fabric

When cutting crumb fabric, start by straightening up one edge. Cut rectangular units as you would a single piece of fabric. Once the piece is cut, it is a good idea to clean up bulk around the edges. Do this by removing any fabric tails, as well as unpicking where there are seams and intersections that would create bulk when adding these pieces to your blocks and units.

Flying geese ruler

A flying geese ruler is an efficient way to cut half-square triangles (HSTs) and quarter-square triangles (QSTs) from crumb fabric.

1 For HSTs, cut a strip of fabric of the width instructed. Line the ruler up with the bottom edge of the strip and cut as shown.

2 Flip the ruler, aligning it with the cut just made as shown. Cut across the strip.

3 Continue in this way until you have the number of HSTs required.

4 For QSTs, cut a strip of fabric of the width instructed. Place the ruler with its tip aligned with the top edge of the strip and cut along both sides of the ruler as shown.

5 Flip the ruler, aligning its tip with the bottom edge of the strip and one side with the cut just made, then cut along the other side of the ruler as shown.

6 Continue in this way until you have the number of QSTs required.

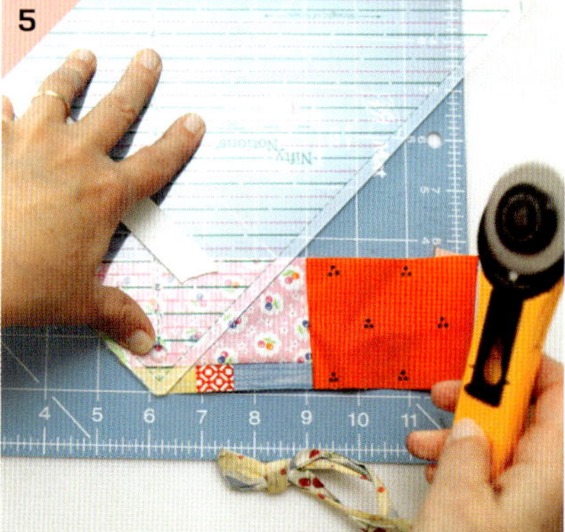

Using an AccuQuilt Fabric Cutter

1 Place two or three pieces of crumb or strip-set fabric on the desired AccuQuilt die.

2 Place the protective sheet that comes with the machine over the fabric and then feed it through the machine.

3 Rub your hand over the protective sheet to release static and slide it off.

4 Enjoy using precisely cut pieces with no dog-ears to remove.

1

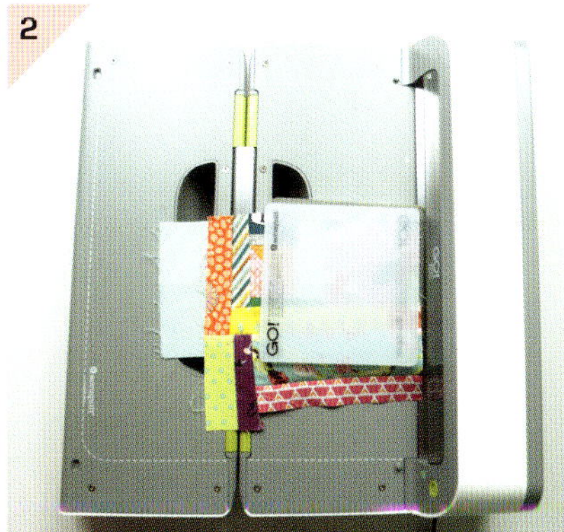
2

4

KISS: Be mindful of the 'layers' added by the seams in your crumb fabric. AccuQuilt Go! fabric cutters can only cut six layers of fabric accurately, which is why I only put two or three layers of crumb or strip-set fabric through the machine at once.

Projects where an AccuQuilt Fabric Cutter can be used

Rainbow Star: AccuQuilt dies #55000 and #55001

Goodnight, Irene: AccuQuilt die #55437

Parella Glam: AccuQuilt die #55000 and #55001

Abundance: AccuQuilt die #50056

Streak of Lightning: AccuQuilt die #55000

SMALL PROJECTS

While small in size these projects pack a punch, allowing your scrappy bits and strips to shine in a variety of ways. Dress up your home with a wall hanging and table runner, or create one of the bags and go out in style.

RAINBOW STAR

Find a home for crumbs of every colour in this cheerful wall hanging. It's sure to brighten any room in your home from a child's bedroom to your creative space.

Approximate size: 24in (61cm) square

MATERIALS

- ½yd (50cm) of background fabric
- At least one 7½in crumb-fabric square in each of the following colours: aqua, dark blue, green, orange, pink, purple, red and yellow
- 28in (71cm) square of backing fabric
- ¼yd (30cm) of binding fabric
- 28in (71cm) square of wadding (batting)

Cutting instructions

Background fabric

- Four 7in squares, each cut once on the diagonal or four AccuQuilt die #55001
- Four 6½in squares or four AccuQuilt die #55000

Crumb fabric

- Cut each colour into a 7in square and cut each square once on the diagonal or cut with AccuQuilt die #55001

Binding fabric

- Three 2½in wide strips across the width of the fabric

KISS: For details about how to make crumb fabric, see Creating the Basics, Making crumb fabric. There will be more interest to your crumb fabric in the various colours if you use a large range of different values within that colour. A simple trick to achieve this is to put your camera on its black and white setting and check to see the range of greys you have. The more shades of grey you have, the more contrast you will have in your crumb fabric.

Pinwheel centre

1 Pair up crumb-fabric triangles as follows:

- one aqua with one dark blue
- one orange with one red
- one purple with one pink
- one yellow with one green

2 Place each pair of crumb-fabric triangles right sides together and sew on the long (diagonal) edge to make four half-square triangles.

3 Open the half-square triangles out and press. Keeping the 45-degree line of your ruler aligned with the diagonal seam, trim each one to 6½in square.

4 Arrange the half-square triangles into two rows of two, making sure you position them as shown. Sew into rows and then sew the rows together. This completes the pinwheel centre, which should measure 12½in square.

Flying geese units

5 Place each remaining crumb-fabric triangle right sides together with a background fabric triangle. Sew each pair together on the long (diagonal) edge. Open out and press. Keeping the 45-degree line of your ruler aligned with the diagonal seam, trim each one to 6½in square. You will have the following half-square triangles:

- one aqua/background
- one dark blue/background
- one green/background
- one orange/background
- one pink/background
- one purple/background
- one red/background
- one yellow/background

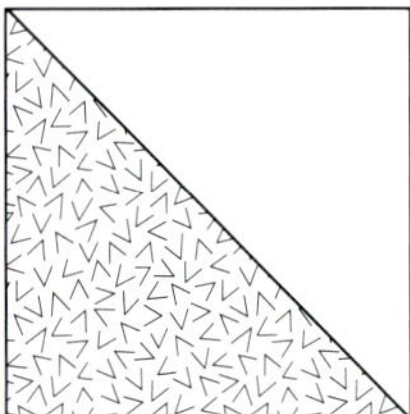

6 Take the orange/background and yellow/background half-square triangles and join to create a flying goose unit. Make sure you orientate the half-square triangles as shown, i.e. so the background fabrics form a central triangle.

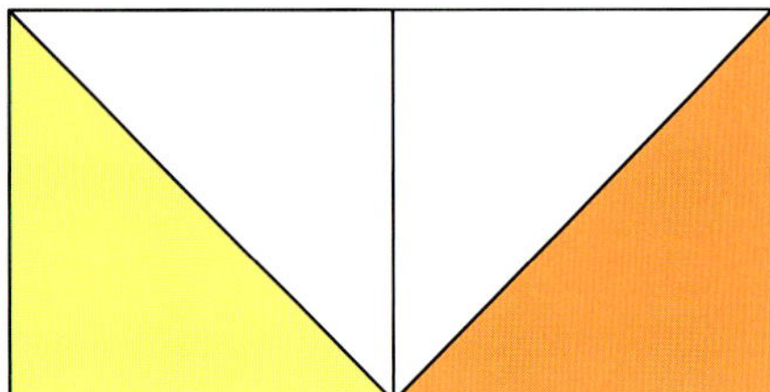

7 Repeat Step 6 to make the following flying geese units, again taking care with the orientations:

- aqua/background half-square triangle with green/ background half-square triangle
- dark blue/background half-square triangle with purple/ background half-square triangle
- pink/background half-square triangle with red/ background half-square triangle

Hanging assembly

8 Referring to the flat shot, arrange the flying geese units around the edges of the pinwheel centre, making sure you match up colours of the crumb-fabric triangles, and then place a 6in background square in each corner.

9 Sew the units into rows and then join the rows to complete the hanging top.

Quilting and finishing

10 Make a quilt sandwich of the hanging top, the wadding (batting) and the backing fabric (see General Techniques, Making a quilt sandwich).

11 Quilt as desired. My hanging was quilted with feathers in each of the star points and then a looping stipple in the background (see General Techniques, Quilting).

12 Square-up and bind to finish (see General Techniques, Squaring-up your quilt and Binding).

Enjoy your wall hanging.

BOLD & BRIGHT

Carry your essentials in style with an eco-friendly courier bag. It allows you to make a statement while helping to save the world.

Approximate size: 9½ x 7¾ x 2in (24 x 20 x 5cm)

MATERIALS

- 9 x 21in made crumb-fabric rectangle (see Creating the Basics, Making crumb fabric)
- ⅝yd (60cm) of contrast fabric
- ⅜yd (40cm) of strap and binding fabric
- 9 x 21in (23 x 54cm) of wadding (batting)
- One 8in (20cm) zipper

Cutting instructions

Contrast fabric

- One 9 x 21in rectangle (backing of crumb outer panel)
- One 3 x 8in rectangle (top outer of zipper panel)
- One 7½ x 8in rectangle (bottom outer of zipper panel)
- One 10 x 8in rectangle (inner of zipper panel)
- Two 3 x 2½in rectangles (lining tabs)
- Two 10 x 2½in rectangles (side panels)
- One 2½ x 8in rectangle (base)

Strap and binding fabric

- One 4in wide strip across the width of the fabric (strap)
- Three 2¼in wide strips across the width of the fabric (binding)

Crumb outer panel

1 Make a quilt sandwich of the crumb-fabric rectangle, the wadding (batting) and the 9 x 21in backing fabric rectangle (see General Techniques, Making a quilt sandwich).

2 Quilt as desired. I quilted organic vertical (short edge to short edge) lines approximately ½in apart.

3 Square-up to 8 x 20in. Set aside.

Zipper panel

4 Take the 3 x 8in contrast rectangle and place it right side up. Open the zipper and, with the zipper pull on the right-hand side, place it right side down on the top 8in edge of the rectangle, matching up the top edge of the zipper tape with the raw edge of the rectangle. Pin in place and stitch, adjusting the zipper pull as you go. Open out and press. Topstitch if desired.

5 Take the 7½ x 8in contrast rectangle and, in the same way as in Step 4, sew the other side of the zipper tape to the top 8in edge of the rectangle. This zipper panel should measure 10 x 8in – trim to size if necessary.

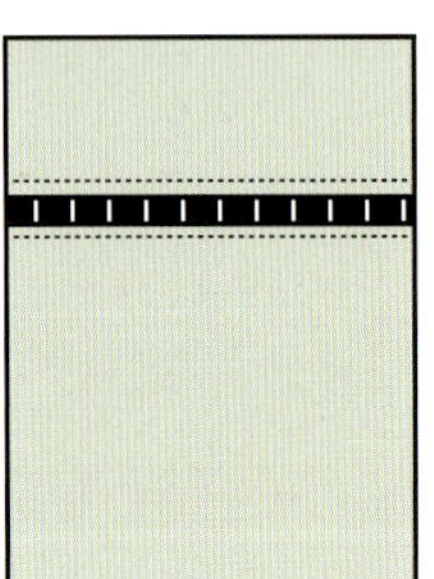

6 Take the 10 x 8in contrast rectangle. Place it right sides together with the outer zipper panel made in Step 5, matching up the raw edges. Sew it in place along the top 8in edge of the outer zipper panel (the raw edge of the narrower (3in) rectangle).

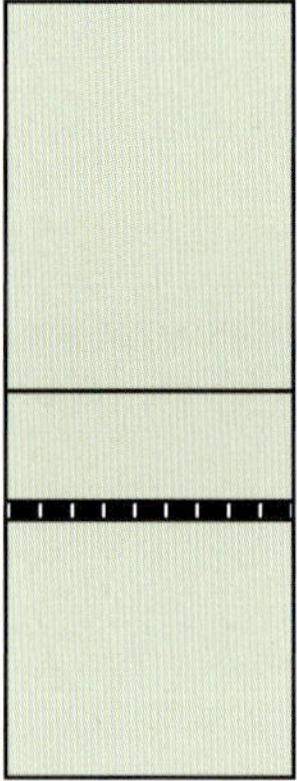

7 Fold the large rectangle over on itself so it is wrong sides together with the outer zipper panel. Match up the raw edges and then press along the seam sewn in Step 6 to make a crisp (top) edge.

8 Topstitch along the folded (top) edge and then baste the side edges. Set aside.

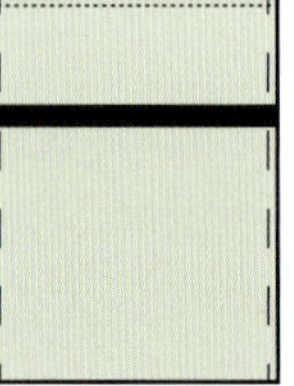

Strap, side and base unit

9 Take the 4in wide strip of strap fabric and, wrong sides together, fold it in half lengthwise and press. Open the strip out and then, wrong sides together, fold each long edge over so they meet at the centre crease.

10 Then fold the strap in half, so the folded edges meet and the raw edges are enclosed. Press. Topstitch down each long edge. This completes the strap.

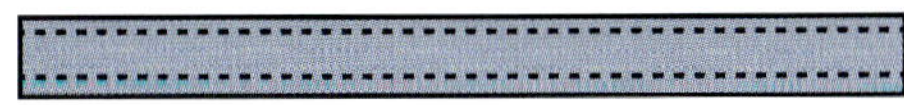

11 Take a 3 x 2½in contrast rectangle and, wrong sides together, fold over ¼in on the top 2½in edge. Press. Fold over another ¼in (which will enclose the raw edge). Press. Repeat with the second 3 x 2½in contrast rectangle.

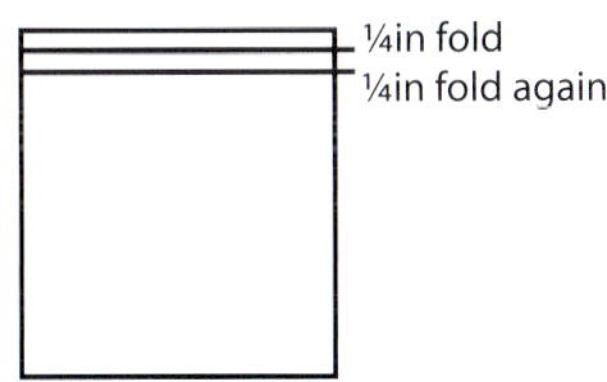

12 Topstitch the folded top edges to secure. These are your lining tabs.

13 Take a 10 x 2½in contrast rectangle and one of the lining tabs made in Step 12. Right sides together, match up the raw 2½in edge of the lining tab with one 2½in edge of the 10 x 2½in rectangle. Matching up the raw edges of the strap with the 2½in raw edges of the lining tab and the rectangle, place one short end of the strap centrally between the lining tab and the rectangle. Stitch these pieces in place, using double stitching where the strap is for extra strength.

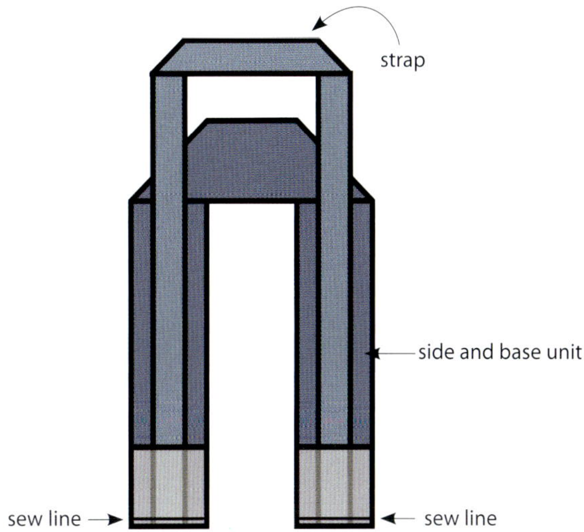

14 Take the 2½ x 8in contrast rectangle and join it to the raw 2½in raw edge (i.e. opposite the strap end) of the unit made in Step 13. Make sure the strap is out of the way before sewing.

15 Take the remaining 10 x 2½in contrast rectangle and the remaining lining tab. In the same manner as in Step 13, taking care not to twist the strap, place the remaining end of the strap between the lining tab and rectangle, and stitch in place as before. Then join this unit to the bag base (the 2½ x 8in contrast rectangle) as in Step 14.

16 Turn the strap ends of the unit made in Step 15 right side out. Press. For each side of the strap, where it joins the sides of the bag, topstitch along the top edge of the contrast fabric (where the strap is sandwiched between the lining tab and the side unit), which will help to secure the strap. This completes the strap, side and base unit.

Bag assembly

17 Take the zipper panel and beginning at the top of one side edge, right sides together and keeping the strap out of the way, pin the strap, side and base unit made in Step 16 in place around the side, bottom edge and the other side of the zipper panel. At the corners, fold the strap, side and base unit back on itself like you would with binding at the corners of a quilt and then continue along the edge. Stitch in place.

18 Starting at the bottom edge of the crumb outer panel, pin the other edge of the strap, side and base unit in place in the same way as in Step 17. Stitch in place. Note that the strap, side and base unit will only go about halfway up each side of the crumb outer panel, as half of the outer panel will form the bag's front flap.

19 Take two of the 2¼in wide binding fabric strips and join into one length using a 45-degree seam. Press the seam open and trim the 'ears'. Wrong sides together, fold the strip in half lengthwise and press. With the bag wrong side out, working from the inside of the bag, use this binding to neaten the seams of the quilted panel, working in the order given: start at the midway point of the bottom back seam and bind to one back corner, bind up the side seam all the way to the top corner of the outer flap, bind the short edge of the outer flap, bind down the other side of the outer flap all the way to the bottom back corner, bind the rest of the bottom back seam. See General Techniques, Binding for how to treat corners and how to join your binding ends at the start/finish point. Fold the binding over to cover the seams and neatly slipstitch the folded edge in place.

20 Take the remaining 2¼in wide binding fabric strip. Wrong sides together, fold over approximately ¼in at the starting short end to neaten, then fold the strip in half lengthwise and press. Working as in Step 19, use this binding strip to neaten the front seams, starting at one top corner, binding to the corresponding bottom corner, then along the bottom front seam and up the other front side seam to the corresponding top corner. Before you get to the end, trim the binding with an approximately ¼in overhang and turn this under as before to neaten. Fold the binding over to cover the seams and neatly slipstitch the folded edge in place.

21 Turn the bag right side out.

Enjoy your bag.

SPRING FLING

Vibrant crumb flowers are combined with striped stems and leaves or grass for a fun and whimsical addition to your spring decorations.

Approximate size: 14½ x 43in (37 x 109cm)

MATERIALS

- ½yd (50cm) of background fabric
- Two 12in crumb-fabric squares
- Thirty green fabric strips 1–2in in width and at least 10in long
- 19 x 51in (48 x 130cm) of backing fabric
- ¼yd (30cm) of binding fabric
- 19 x 51in (48 x 130cm) of wadding (batting)

Cutting instructions

Background fabric

- Seven 2 x 5½in rectangles
- Seven 5½ x 8½in rectangles
- Twenty-eight 2in squares
- Eight 1½ x 14½in rectangles

Crumb fabric

- Seven 5½in squares

Binding fabric

- Three 2½in wide strips across the width of the fabric

KISS: For details about how to make crumb fabric, see Creating the Basics, Making crumb fabric.

Flower head units

1 Draw a diagonal line from corner to corner on the wrong side of each of the twenty-eight 2in background squares.

2 Take one of these marked background squares and one 5½in crumb square. Right sides together, place the background square on top of one corner of the crumb square, with the diagonal line running from outer edge to outer edge of the crumb square. Sew on the marked line.

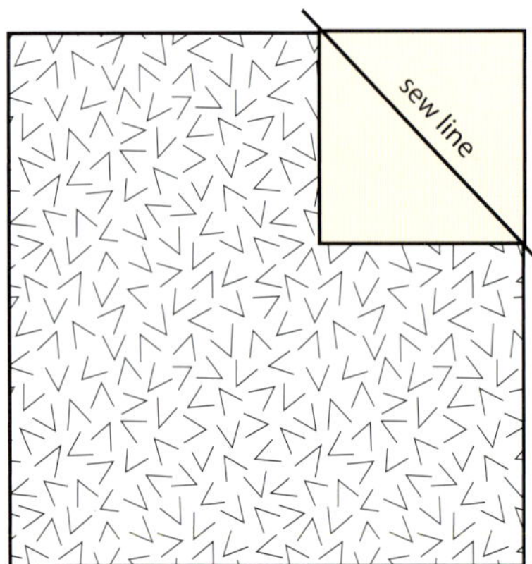

3 Flip the background square open to check the corner of the crumb square is covered. If it isn't, unpick and redo Step 2. If the corner is covered, flip the background square back and trim ¼in beyond the stitched line, flip it open again and press.

4 Repeat Steps 2 and 3 on the other three corners of the crumb square.

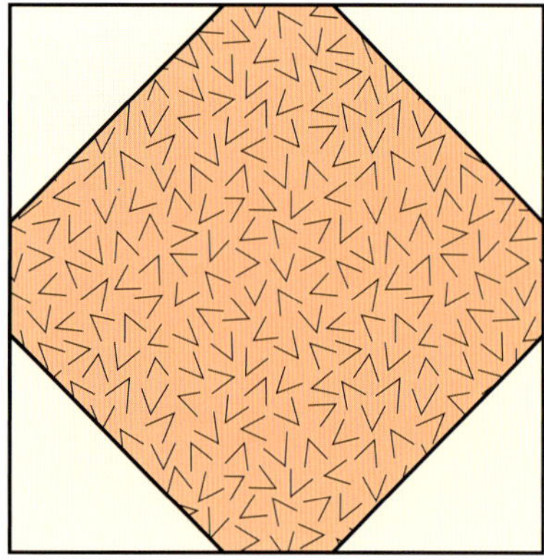

5 Repeat Steps 2–4 with the remaining 2in background squares and 5½in crumb squares.

6 Sew a 2 x 5½in background rectangle to the edge you want to be the top of each unit to create seven flower head units.

Strip-set units

7 Sew the green fabric strips and strings into strip sets that are 9in wide. Make two or three strip sets for variety. See Creating the Basics, Making a strip/string set.

KISS: If you use long and short strips in each strip set you can rearrange them, which enables you to create greater variety without having to make lots of different strip sets.

8 Subcut the strip sets into eighteen 1–1¾in wide strip sets.

Stems with grass units

9 Take a 5½ x 8½in background rectangle and make an angled cut from short edge to short edge near the centre for the stem.

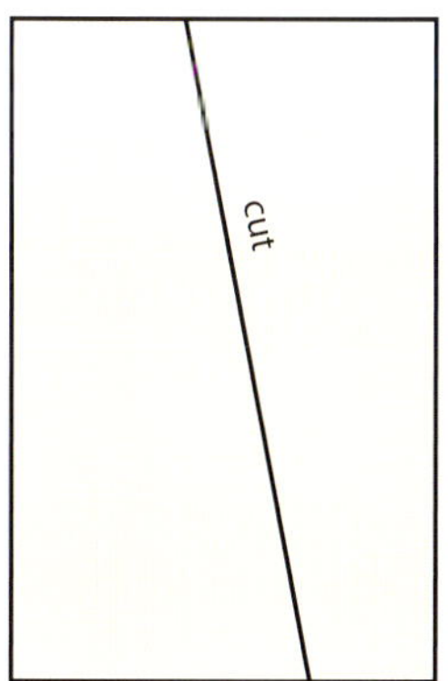

10 Insert a green strip set between the cut edges to create the stem of the flower.

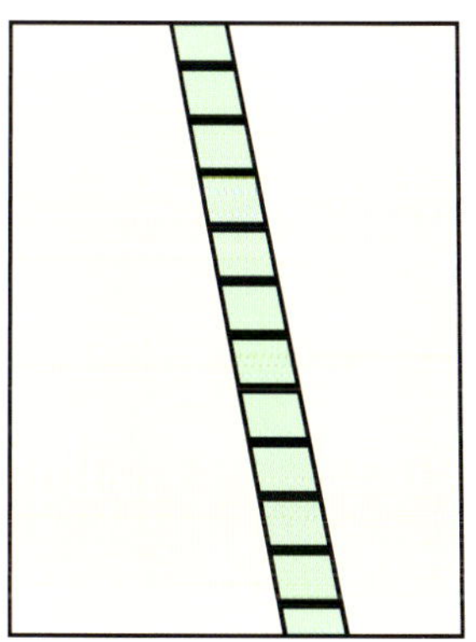

11 Make a cut from the bottom edge to partially up the side edge on each side of the stem for the grass.

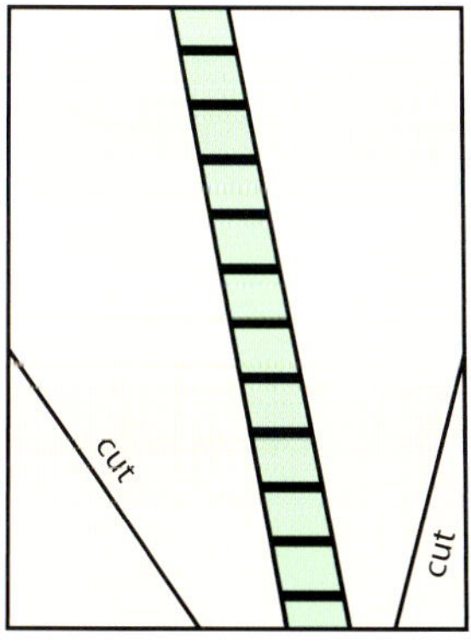

12 Insert a green strip set between each of the cut edges to create the grass.

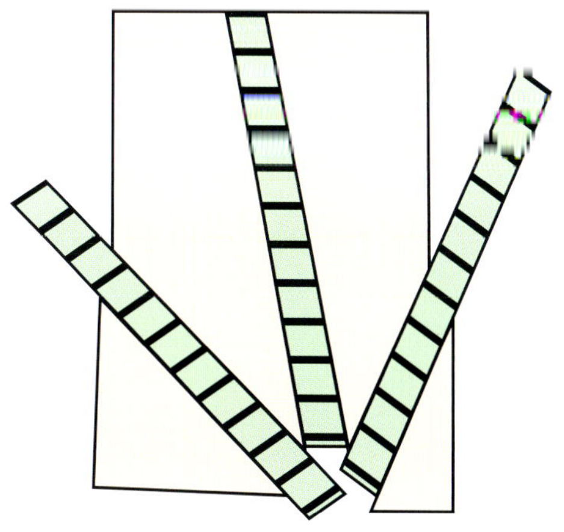

13 Square-up the unit so it measures 5½ x 8in.

14 Repeat Steps 9–13 with three more of the 5½ x 8in background rectangles. If you wish you can make some of the grass cuts so they cut into the stem a little. You will have four stems with grass units.

KISS: When squaring up the Stems with grass units (Step 13) and Stems with leaves units (Step 18), and trimming the Stems with leaves units (Step 17), save the strip set offcuts as you may be able to use them in other units. You can join offcuts of the same width to make longer strip sets if necessary.

Stems with leaves units

15 Take a 5½ x 8½in background rectangle and make an angled cut from short edge to short edge near the centre for the stem, and then make an additional cut from the stem to the side edge on each side of the stem for the leaves.

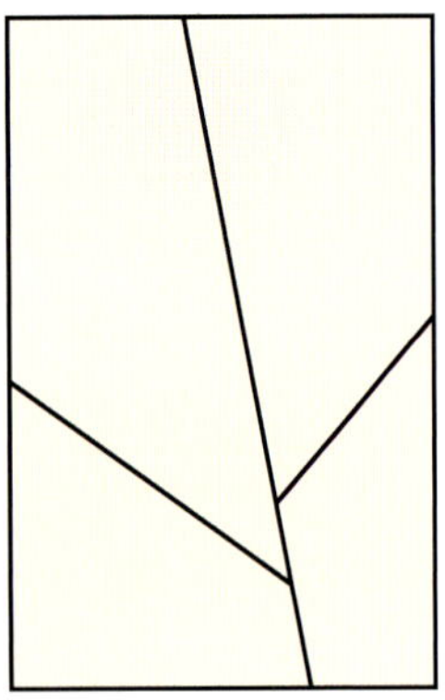

16 Insert a green strip set between each of the short cut edges to create the leaves.

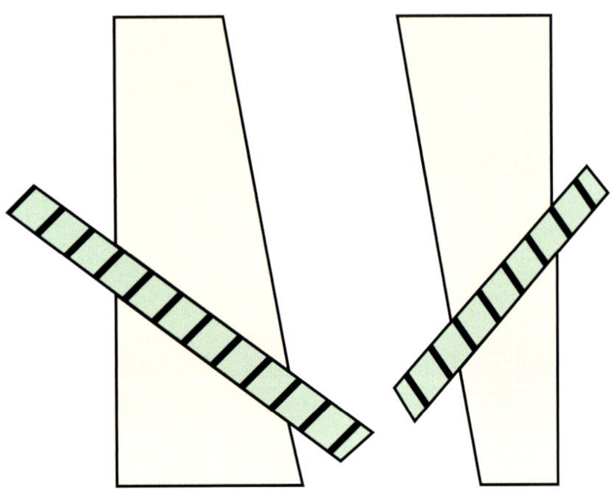

17 Trim to straighten up the edges and then insert a green strip set between the long cut edges to create the stem of the flower.

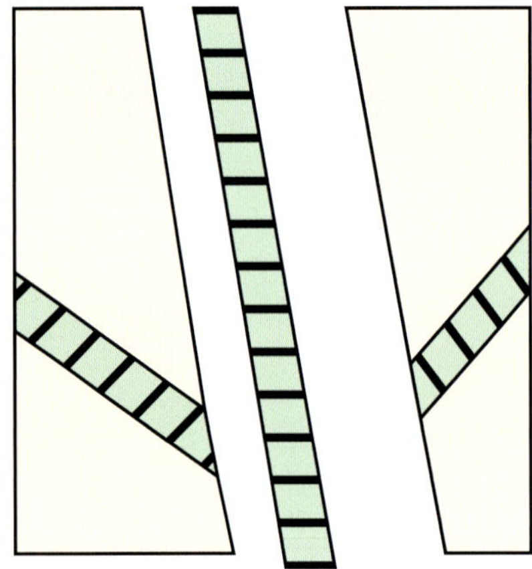

18 Square-up the unit so it measures 5½ x 8in.

19 Repeat Steps 15–18 with the remaining 5½ x 8½in background rectangles, varying the direction of the stem cut. You will have three stems with leaves units.

Runner assembly

20 Sew a stem unit to the bottom of each flower unit, taking care to attach it the correct way round.

21 Arrange the flower and stem units in a row, with a flower with leaves unit in the centre and at each end, and with two flower with grass units either side of the centre unit, making sure you alternate the units flower head up, flower head down, etc. (three will face one way and four the other way round).

22 Sew a 1½ x 14½in background rectangle between each flower unit as you sew the units into a row.

23 Sew a 1½ x 14½in background rectangle to either end of the row to complete the runner top.

Quilting and finishing

24 Make a quilt sandwich of the runner top, the wadding (batting) and the backing fabric (see General Techniques, Making a quilt sandwich).

25 Quilt as desired. My runner was quilted with parallel wavy lines and swirls running vertically through the flower units (i.e. running from long edge to long edge of the runner) (see General Techniques, Quilting).

26 Square-up and bind to finish (see General Techniques, Squaring-up your quilt and Binding).

Enjoy your runner.

FREE TO ROAM

This is one of my favourite bags to make. I love how fun and easy it is to put together and to use. Fill it, pull it and you're good to go!

Approximate size: 8in (20cm) high x 5in (12.5cm) diameter

MATERIALS

- Two 8 x 7½in made crumb-fabric rectangles (see Creating the Basics, Making crumb fabric) or two 8 x 7½in strip-set rectangles (see Creating the Basics, Making a strip/string set) for outer bag
- One fat quarter of lining and base fabric
- One 5½in (14cm) square of wadding (batting)
- 1¼yds (1.2m) of ½in (1.25cm) wide ribbon or cotton tape, or hemp twine cord

Cutting instructions

Lining and base fabric

- Two 8 x 7½in rectangles (bag lining)
- Two Circle templates (bag base)

Ribbon or tape

- Two 20in long pieces
- Bias tape (optional)

Bag body

1 Take the 8 x 7½in outer bag rectangles and place them right sides together. Measure and mark 1¼in down from the top corner on each side (8in side) of the top rectangle. In the same way, make a second mark on each side 1¾in down from the top corners.

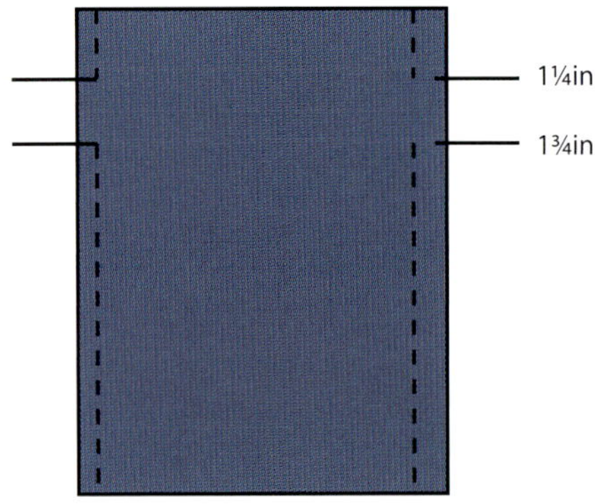

2 Using a ¼in seam, on one side of the rectangles sew from the top corner to the first (1¼in) mark, stop, take a few reverse stitches to strengthen. Then sew from the second (1¾in) mark, taking a few reverse stitches when you start sewing, to the bottom corner. Repeat on the other side.

3 Press each seam open. Turn right side out and stitch a scant ⅛in all around the open slit on each side, which will finish the edge and add strength.

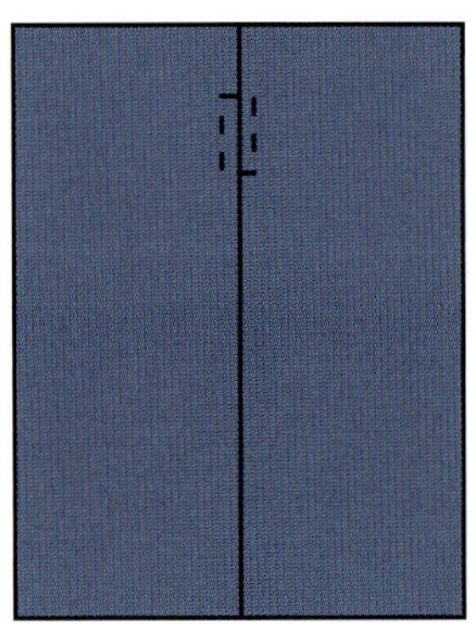

4 Place the 8 x 7½in bag lining rectangles right sides together and join by sewing down each side (8in) edge. Press each seam open.

5 With the outer bag right side out and the bag lining wrong side out, place the outer bag inside the bag lining – right sides will be facing each other. Match up the side seams and the midway points between the side seams, making sure the open slits are nearest the top edge. Pin in place and then, using a ¼in seam, sew all around the top edge. When you get back to where you started, overlap the stitching for a short distance to secure the seam.

6 Pull the lining up and press the seam towards the lining.

7 Fold the lining over so it is inside the bag – wrong sides will now be facing each other. Match up the side seams and the midway points between the side seams, and make sure the lining is neatly in place. Press around the top to give a crips edge, and then topstitch all around the bag ⅛in down from the top edge. Also topstitch all around the bag 1in and 1½in down from the top edge – this creates a channel for the drawstring ribbon/tape.

Bag base

8 Make a quilt sandwich of a base Circle, the wadding (batting) and the other base Circle (see General Techniques, Making a quilt sandwich).

9 Quilt a cross (i.e. a north–south line and an east–west line) as shown to hold layers together.

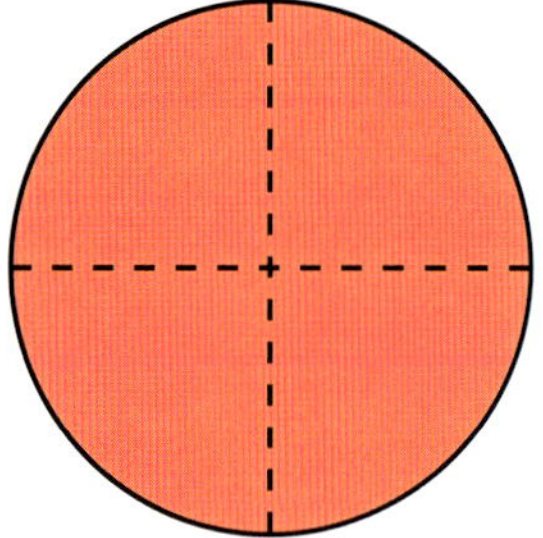

Constructing the bag

10 With the bag body lining side out, take the bag base and match up the ends of one of the quilted lines with the bag's side seams. Match up the ends of the other quilted line with the midway points between the side seams. Pin in place and then, using a ¼in seam, sew all around the base. You can leave this seam as is or cover it with bias tape to hide the raw edges. Turn the bag right side out.

11 Take one 20in piece of ribbon/tape/twine cord. Put a safety pin at one end and then feed it into one side slit and all around the drawstring channel, taking care not to twist it, until it come out at the same side slit. Remove the safety pin and tie off ends of ribbon/tape.

12 Repeat Step 11 with the other 20in piece of ribbon/tape/twine cord, starting and ending at the slit on the other side of the bag.

Enjoy your bag.

CRUMB PROJECTS

No fabric scrap is too small when creating crumb fabric. These projects allow you to showcase your one-of-a-kind fabrics in vibrant quilts that draw on traditions but with a contemporary twist.

BLOOM

Bloom is the result of an overflowing low-volume scrap bin and the hope of a granddaughter. I have two grandsons now, but no granddaughters. Though families have a way of growing and there is always hope.

Approximate size: 48in (122cm) square

MATERIALS

- Sixteen 12½in made crumb-fabric squares (see Creating the Basics, Making crumb fabric)
- Orange and yellow scraps, at least 5in wide – I used five different fabrics, each 5 x 8in (see Cutting instructions)
- Blue, pink and purple scraps, at least 3in wide – I used five different fabrics, each 3 x 7in (see Cutting instructions)
- Four green scraps, at least 5in wide – four 5 x 5in charm squares would be ideal
- 1¼yds (1.2m) of light green jumbo rickrack
- 1¼yds (1.2m) of dark green regular rickrack
- ¼yd (25cm) of lightweight fusible interfacing
- 56in (142cm) square of backing fabric
- ½yd (50cm) of binding fabric
- 56in (142cm) square of wadding (batting)

Cutting instructions

Orange and yellow scraps

- A total of twenty large Dresden templates – I cut four templates from each of my five fabrics
- A total of four 3in squares

Blue, pink and purple scraps

- Twenty small Dresden templates of each colour – I cut four templates from each of my five fabrics
- Four 2½in squares of each colour

Rickrack – jumbo and regular

- One 17½in length of each
- One 13in length of each
- One10½in length of each

Binding fabric

- Six 2½in wide strips across the width of the fabric

Quilt background

1 Take the 12½in made crumb-fabric squares and arrange into four rows of four squares each.

2 Sew the squares into rows and then join the rows. This completes your quilt background. Set aside.

Dresden rings

3 Take an orange/yellow large Dresden template and fold it in half lengthwise, right sides together.

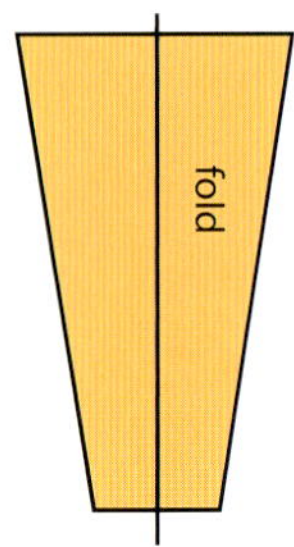

4 Press. Then sew along the top edge (the wider short end).

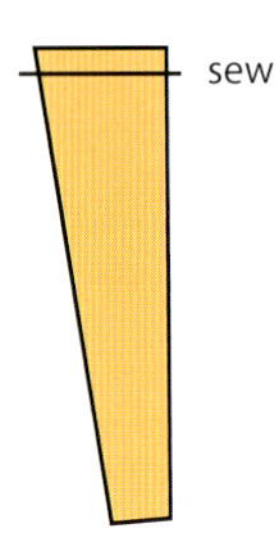

5 Clip the corner (at the folded edge), taking care not to snip into your stitching. Finger-press the seam open.

6 Turn right side out. Use a Purple Thang (see Tools & Materials) or a capped pen to make sure the corner is turned out neatly.

7 On the wrong side, match up the end of the seam with the central fold mark to create a Dresden blade. Press. You may wish to press again from the right side of the blade.

8 Repeat Steps 3–7 with the remaining orange/yellow large Dresden templates to make a total of twenty Dresden blades.

9 Arrange the blades into a ring with the points of the blades pointing outwards (refer to flat shot).

10 Take two blades and place them right sides together. Sew together on one side seam. Open out and press the seam to one side. Repeat with another pair of blades. Join the pairs together and then add a fifth blade to complete one-quarter of the ring.

11 Repeat Step 10 to make a second quarter of the ring. Join the quarters together to make half a ring.

12 Repeat Steps 10 and 11 to make the second half of the ring. Join the two half rings to complete the full orange/yellow ring.

13 Working on one colour at a time, repeat Steps 3–12 with the blue, pink and purple small Dresden templates to make one blue, one pink and one purple full ring.

Dresden centres

14 Take the four orange/yellow 3in squares. Join them into two rows of two squares each and then join the rows to create a four-patch unit.

15 Trace the Circle template onto lightweight cardboard and cut out on the drawn line. Centre the template on the wrong side of the four-patch unit and trace around the circle. Sew a line of basting stitches ⅛in beyond the drawn line. Cut the circle out ¼in beyond the line of basting stitches. Start to pull the basting stitches so the circle begins to close in on itself. Insert the cardboard template into the circle against the wrong side of the fabric, matching up the template with the drawn line, and continue to pull the basting stitches until the template is firmly enclosed in the circle. Make sure there are no gathers around the edge of the circle and then press with steam and/or starch. Once you have a crisp firm edge, pop out the cardboard template and then press the fabric circle again. This completes the orange/yellow Dresden centre. (See Circle preparation in Creating the Basics, Machine appliqué.)

16 Repeat Steps 14 and 15 with the blue, pink and purple 2½in squares to make one blue, one pink and one purple Dresden centre.

Leaves

Refer to Appliqué in Creating the Basics, Machine appliqué when making the leaves.

17 Trace four Leaf templates onto the non-fusible side of the lightweight fusible interfacing, leaving space to cut out with at least ½in all around each shape.

18 With the fusible side of the interfacing against the right side of the fabric, place a leaf shape onto one of your green scraps. Pin in place and then stitch on the drawn line of the leaf shape. Cut the leaf out ¼in beyond the stitched line. Clip the tips of the leaves, taking care not to snip into your stitching.

19 Cut a small slit in the interfacing, taking care not to cut the fabric, too. Turn the leaf right side out through the slit. Use a Purple Thang (see Tools & Materials) or a capped pen to push out the points, and also to run along the seams to make crisp edges. I find a wallpaper roller is great for achieving a crisp edge.

20 Repeat Steps 18 and 19 to make a total of four leaves.

Appliquéing the quilt top

Refer to the quilt flat shot when adding the appliqué.

21 Take your quilt background and find the centre point of the bottom edge. Take the 17½in length of jumbo rickrack and, matching up one short end of the rickrack with the centre point of the bottom of the quilt, run it vertically up the quilt. Pin in place and then attach it to the quilt top by sewing through the middle of the rickrack from short end to short end.

22 Take one of your leaves and place it approximately 4½in up from the bottom on the left-hand side of the rickrack stem – the rickrack should overlap the inner tip of the leaf. Press in place and then topstitch all around the outer edge of the leaf.

23 In the same manner as in Step 22, add a second leaf to the stem, this time approximately 11in up from the bottom on the right-hand side of the stem.

24 Topstitch down both long edges of jumbo rickrack.

25 Take the 17½in length of regular rickrack and place it down the centre of the jumbo rickrack. Attach it in place by sewing through the middle of the rickrack from short end to short end.

26 Using the same process as in Steps 21–25, make a stem 12in in from the bottom left-hand corner of the quilt top. This time use the 10½in lengths of jumbo and regular rickrack and place a leaf approximately 5½in up from the bottom on the left-hand side of the rickrack stem.

27 Using the same process as in Steps 21–25, make a stem 12in in from the bottom right-hand corner of the quilt top. This time use the 13in lengths of jumbo and regular rickrack and place a leaf approximately 6¼in up from the bottom on the right-hand side of the rickrack stem.

28 Centre a small Dresden flower ring over the top of each stem, overlapping the stem by approximately ½in – you can follow my arrangement of colours or choose your own. Pin or glue in place and then topstitch all around the outer edge of each flower.

29 Centre the corresponding Dresden centre in the middle of each flower. Pin or glue in place and then topstitch all around the outer edge of each centre.

30 Position the orange/yellow Dresden sun ring at the top left of the quilt centre with the top of the sun 4½in down from the quilt's top edge and the left-hand side of the sun 4½in in from the quilt's left-hand edge. Pin or glue in place and then topstitch all around the outer edge of the sun.

31 Centre the orange/yellow Dresden centre in the middle of the sun. Pin or glue in place and then topstitch all around the outer edge.

Quilting and finishing

32 Make a quilt sandwich of the quilt top, the wadding (batting) and the backing fabric (see General Techniques, Making a quilt sandwich).

33 Quilt as desired. My quilt was quilted with an allover stipple pattern in the background areas and loops in the sun and flowers, and echo quilting around the stems and leaves (see General Techniques, Quilting).

34 Square-up and bind to finish (see General Techniques, Squaring-up your quilt and Binding).

Enjoy your quilt.

GOODNIGHT, IRENE

Giant hexies in a sea of navy and black makes for one jazzy grandmother's garden. I'm a lover of jazz and if you haven't heard 'Goodnight, Irene' sung by Lead Belly you should give it a listen.

Approximate size: 65 x 76in (165 x 193cm)

MATERIALS

- Background – an assortment of black and navy prints, at least 4½in wide (I also threw a few made crumb-fabric units into the mix), totalling approximately 3¾yds (3.5m)
- Flower centres (green) – enough made crumb fabric to cut fourteen Half-hexie templates (see KISS below)
- Flowers (aqua, orange, pink, purple, red, white and yellow) – enough made crumb fabric to cut twelve Half-hexie templates (see KISS below)
- 73 x 84in (185 x 213cm) of backing fabric
- ¾yd (70cm) of binding fabric
- 73 x 84in (185 x 213cm) of wadding (batting)

Cutting instructions

ACCUQUILT GO! 55437

Background fabric

- One hundred and eighteen Half-hexie templates or one hundred and eighteen AccuQuilt die #55437. Cut eighteen of these Half-hexies in half as shown

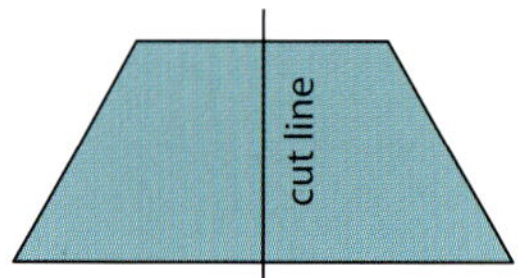

Green crumb fabric

- Fourteen Half-hexie templates or fourteen AccuQuilt die #55437

Each of the other crumb fabrics

- Twelve Half-hexie templates or twelve AccuQuilt die #55437

Binding fabric

- Eight 2½in wide strips across the width of the fabric

KISS: For details about how to make crumb fabric, see Creating the Basics, Making crumb fabric. If you make crumb-fabric rectangles 4½in wide by at least 12in long, you can cut out your first Half-hexie template. Then sew another 4½in wide crumb-fabric rectangle onto the straight 4½in edge of the unused piece, flip the template over and cut out another Half-hexie. Continue in this manner until you have the desired number of Half-hexies. Working this way is the most efficient use of your made crumb fabric and will save waste.

Piecing the quilt top

Follow the layout diagram when constructing the quilt top. Note each row starts and ends with a background half Half-hexie (i.e. a Half-hexie that that has been cut in half).

1 To join the units, place two units right sides together as shown, making sure to leave ¼in of point at the top edge.

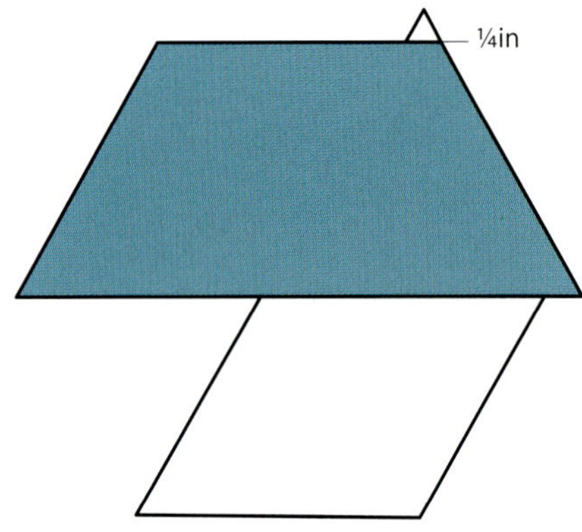

2 Sew the units together, flip open and press.

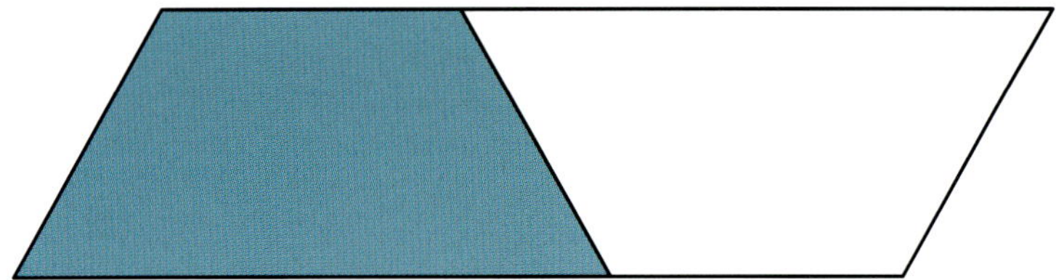

KISS: On odd-numbered rows, press the seams to the left and on even-numbered rows press the seams to the right, then when the rows are joined the seam intersections will nestle together neatly.

3 Working as described in Steps 1 and 2, join the half Half-hexies and Half-hexies into eighteen rows.

4 Join the rows to complete the quilt top. Square-up if necessary.

Quilting and finishing

5 Make a quilt sandwich of the quilt top, the wadding (batting) and the backing fabric (see General Techniques, Making a quilt sandwich).

6 Quilt as desired. My quilt was quilted with an allover floral design (see General Techniques, Quilting).

7 Square-up and bind to finish (see General Techniques, Squaring-up your quilt and Binding).

Enjoy your quilt.

Row 1
Row 2
Row 3
Row 4
Row 5
Row 6
Row 7
Row 8
Row 9
Row 10
Row 11
Row 12
Row 13
Row 14
Row 15
Row 16
Row 17
Row 18

JACKS

As a child I played jacks. My mum was extremely good at the game. I was better at just spinning the jacks and seeing how many I could get spinning at once. However you play, Jacks is sure to delight.

Approximate size: 48in (122cm) square

MATERIALS

- 2½yds (2.3m) of background and border fabric (includes binding)
- Enough made crumb fabric to cut one hundred Wedge templates (see Made crumb-fabric wedges)
- Various scrappy prints, totalling approximately ¾yd (70cm)
- 56in (142cm) square of wadding (batting)

Cutting instructions

Background fabric

- Eight 4½in wide strips across the width of the fabric. Subcut into one hundred Wedge templates

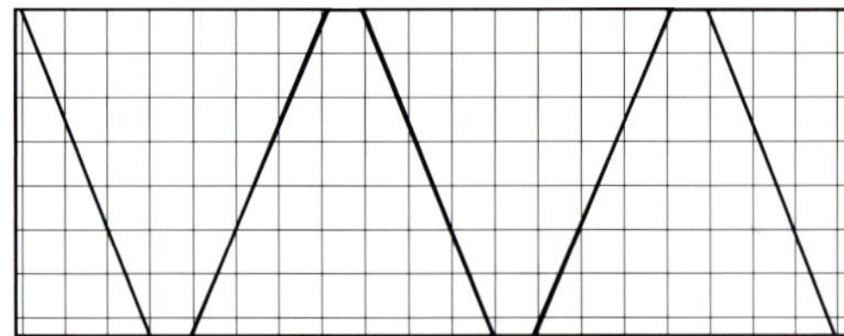

- Forty 1½ x 8½in rectangles (sashing strips)
- Five 2½in wide strips across the width of the fabric. Sew end to end and then subcut into two 2½ x 44½in strips (top and bottom borders) and two 2½ x 48½in strips (side borders)
- Six 2½in wide strips across the width of the fabric (binding)

Scrappy prints

- Fifty 3½in squares, each cut once on the diagonal
- Sixteen 1½in squares

Made crumb-fabric wedges

1 Make around twenty-five 4½ x 13in crumb-fabric rectangles (see Creating the Basics, Making crumb fabric).

2 Cut as many Wedge templates as you can from one crumb-fabric rectangle. Sew any unused rectangle to the next crumb-fabric rectangle on the 4½in edge and then cut as many Wedge templates as you can from this new rectangle.

3 Continue working in this way until you have one hundred Wedge templates. If required, make a few more 4½ x 13in crumb-fabric rectangles.

KISS: Choose scrappy prints for the triangles for your block corners and the squares for the sashing strip rows that are in the same tones and values as those found in your made crumb fabric. Make sure they all contrast with the background fabric to ensure the quilt pattern doesn't get lost.

Kaleidoscope blocks

4 Take one background Wedge and one crumb Wedge. Place them right sides together as shown. Note how they are orientated and that they are offset by ¼in on the (long) edge to be joined.

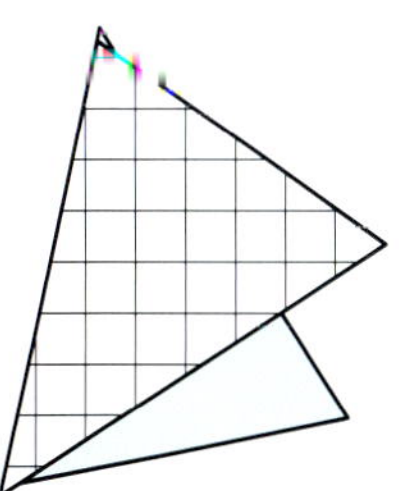

5 Sew together. Flip open and press the seam towards the background fabric.

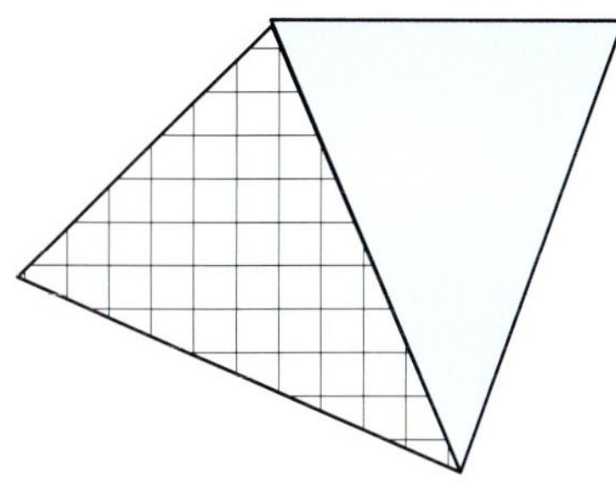

6 Repeat Steps 4 and 5 to make a total of four identical Wedge pairs.

7 Take two Wedge pairs and join as shown to make a half-octagon. Repeat with the two remaining Wedge pairs.

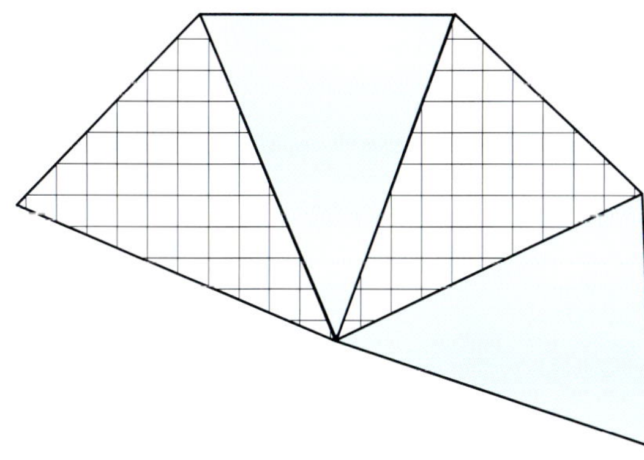

8 Join the two half-octagons as shown to create one complete octagon.

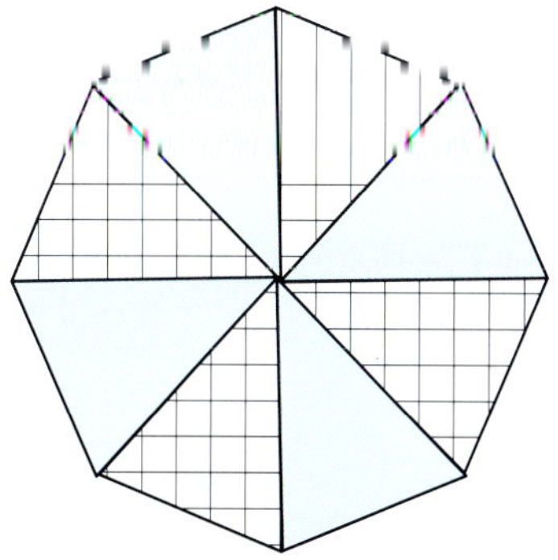

9 Sew a scrappy print triangle to the end of each crumb Wedge as shown. This completes one kaleidoscope block, which should measure 8½in square.

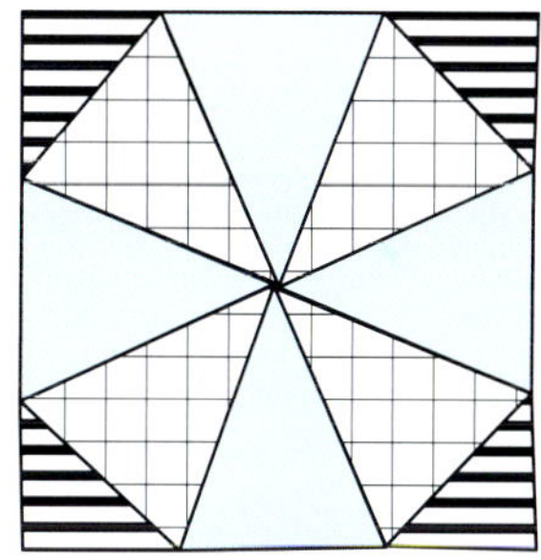

10 Repeat Steps 4–9 to make a total of twenty-five kaleidoscope blocks.

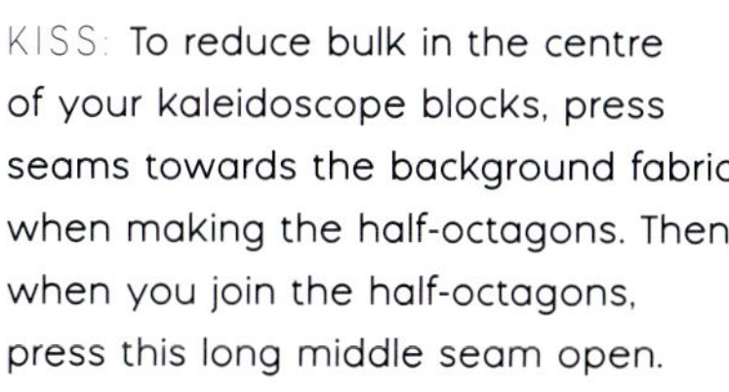

KISS: To reduce bulk in the centre of your kaleidoscope blocks, press seams towards the background fabric when making the half-octagons. Then, when you join the half-octagons, press this long middle seam open.

Quilt assembly

Follow the layout diagram when constructing the quilt top.

11 Arrange your kaleidoscope blocks into five rows of five blocks each with a 1½ x 8½in background sashing rectangle between each block.

12 Sew the blocks and rectangles into rows.

13 Between each block row, arrange five 1½ x 8½in background sashing rectangles with a 1½in scrappy print square between each rectangle. You will have four sashing strip rows in total.

14 Sew the sashing strip rows together. Then join the block and sashing strip rows to complete the quilt centre.

15 Sew a 2½ x 44½in background border strip to the top and bottom of the quilt centre.

16 Sew a 2½ x 48½in background border strip to each side of the quilt centre. This completes your quilt top.

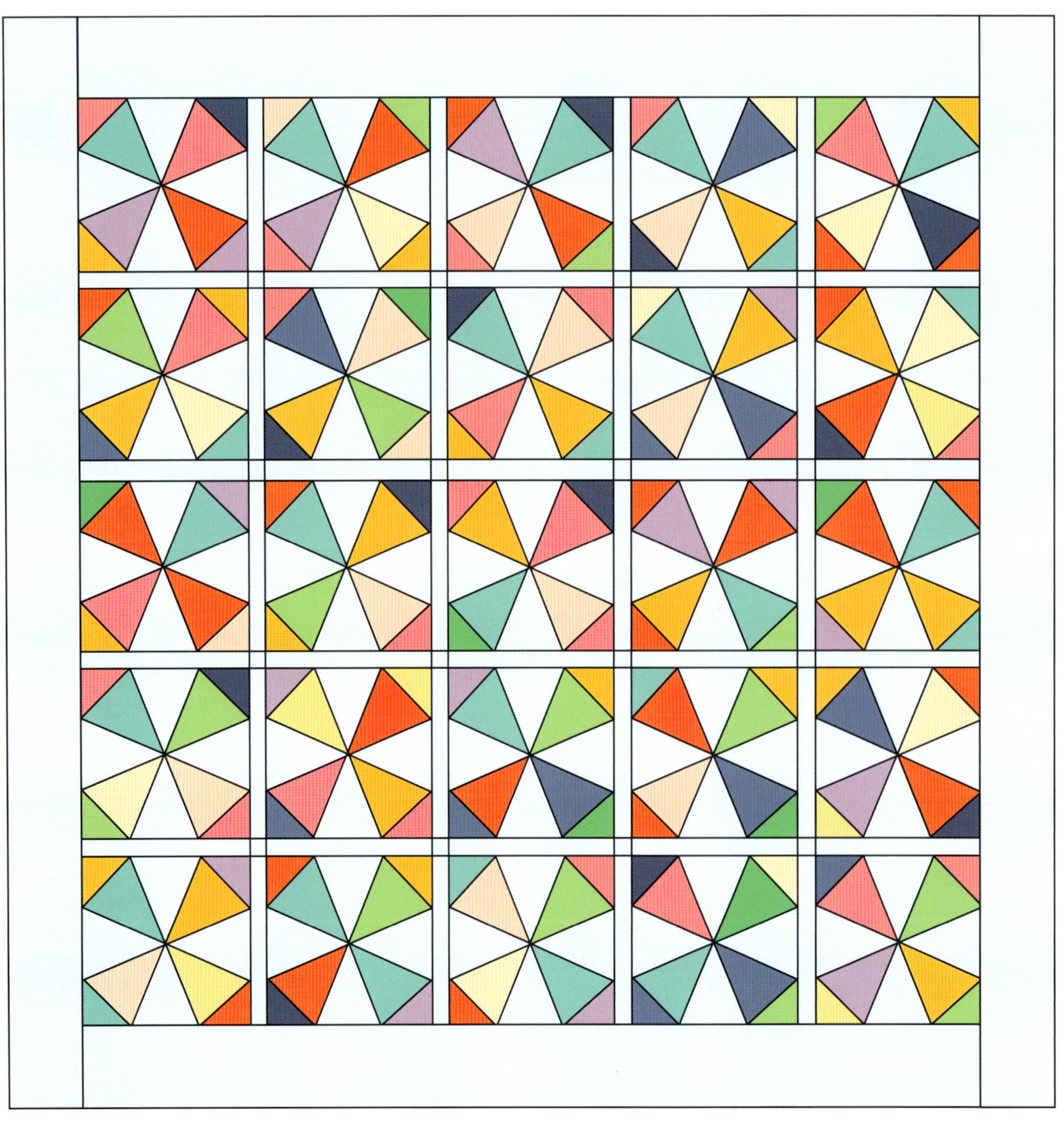

Quilting and finishing

17 Make a quilt sandwich of the quilt top, the wadding (batting) and the backing fabric (see General Techniques, Making a quilt sandwich).

18 Quilt as desired. My quilt was quilted with a large swirl spiralling out into each of the wedges from the centre point, with a meandering vine with swirls quilted through the sashing (see General Techniques, Quilting).

19 Square-up and bind to finish (see General Techniques, Squaring-up your quilt and Binding).

Enjoy your quilt.

PARELLA GLAM

This quilt got its name from my sister, Julie, thanks to her love of maths and a creative play on words. Half-square triangles are joined to make cascading parallelograms of colourful crumb fabric.

Approximate size: 60 x 54in (152 x 137cm)

MATERIALS

- 1⅞yds (1.7m) of background fabric
- Forty crumb-fabric squares, each at least 7in square
- 68 x 62in (173 x 157cm) of backing fabric
- ½yd (50cm) of binding fabric
- 68 x 62in (173 x 157cm) of wadding (batting)

Cutting instructions

ACCUQUILT GO! 55001 55000

Background fabric

- Forty 7in squares or forty AccuQuilt die #55001
- Ten 6½in squares or ten AccuQuilt die #55000

Crumb fabric

- Cut each square into a 7in square or cut with AccuQuilt die #55001

Binding fabric

- Six 2½in wide strips across the width of the fabric

KISS: For details about how to make crumb fabric, see Creating the Basics, Making crumb fabric. When making the crumb fabric for this quilt, I used bright happy crumbs with a wide range of values from dark to very light. Playing with value in your crumb fabric will give it more interest.

Half-square triangles using 7in squares

Two methods are described for making the half-square triangles. If you have used AccuQuilt die #55001 to cut your fabric, follow Steps 5–7; otherwise, follow Steps 1–4.

1 Draw a diagonal line from corner to corner on the wrong side of each of the 7in background squares.

2 Take one background square and one crumb square. Place them right sides together with the marked square on top. Sew ¼in either side of the drawn line. Cut through both layers on the marked line.

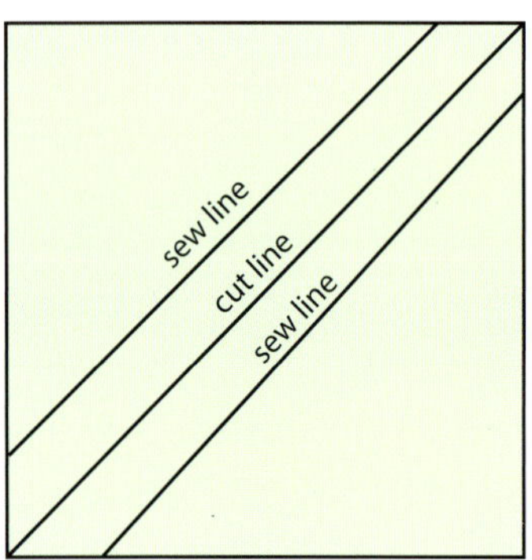

3 Open the half-square triangles out and press. Keeping the 45-degree line of your ruler aligned with the diagonal seam, trim each one to 6½in square.

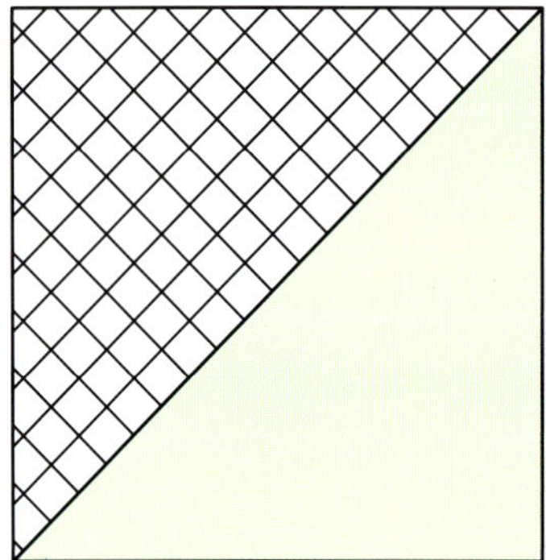

4 Repeat Steps 2 and 3 with your remaining 7in background and crumb squares. You will have eighty half-square triangles.

KISS: **Instead of using crumb fabric you could use scrappy strip sets to make your half-square triangles.**

Half-square triangles using AccuQuilt triangles

5 Place a background AccuQuilt triangle and crumb AccuQuilt triangle right sides together. Sew on the long (diagonal) edge to make one half-square triangle.

6 Half-square triangles made using the AccuQuilt do not need to be trimmed. Simply press the seam towards the background fabric.

7 Repeat Steps 5 and 6 with your remaining background and crumb AccuQuilt triangles. You will have eighty half-square triangles.

Quilt assembly

Follow the layout diagram when constructing the quilt top.

8 Arrange your half-square triangles and 6½in background squares into ten rows of nine units each as shown. Note the orientations of the half-square triangles, and the placement of the background squares in the top and bottom rows.

9 Sew the units into rows and then join the rows. This completes your quilt top.

Quilting and finishing

10 Make a quilt sandwich of the quilt top, the wadding (batting) and the backing fabric (see General Techniques, Making a quilt sandwich).

11 Quilt as desired. My quilt was quilted with feathers in the background fabric areas and a modified orange peel design was quilted in the crumb fabric areas (see General Techniques, Quilting).

12 Square-up and bind to finish (see General Techniques, Squaring-up your quilt and Binding).

Enjoy your quilt.

STRIP PROJECTS

Scrappy strips are combined in a variety of ways to create striking quilts that are bold in looks while being perfect for cuddling with those you love.

FLOW

Go with the flow and just relax with cool blue, green and purple fabric strips sewn together in a spiral-style braid.

Approximate size: 72 x 81in (183 x 206cm)

MATERIALS

- 2¼yds (2.1m) of background fabric
- Scrappy prints, totalling approximately 3½yds (3.2m) – see Cutting instructions
- 3yds (2.8m) foundation fabric – foundation paper or lightweight calico (muslin)
- 80 x 89in (203 x 226cm) of backing fabric
- ⅝yd (60cm) of binding fabric
- 80 x 89in (203 x 226cm) of wadding (batting)

KISS: I prefer to use a permanent foundation (calico (muslin)) when using this method. I like it because it means I don't have to remove foundation paper later, which I find messy and time-consuming. But if you prefer not to add bulk to your quilt then a removable foundation is the one for you.

Cutting instructions

Background fabric

- Thirteen 3½in squares, each cut once on the diagonal to give twenty-six 3½in background triangles
- Nineteen 3½in wide strips across the width of the fabric. Sew end to end and subcut into the following rectangles:
  - One 3½ x12½in
  - Two 3½ x15½in
  - Two 3½ x 24½in
  - Two 3½ x 33½in
  - Two 3½ x 42½in
  - Two 3½ x 51½in
  - Two 3½ x 60½in
  - Two 3½ x 69½in
  - One 3½ x 72½in
  - One 3½ x 78½in

Scrappy prints

- Seven 3in squares, each cut once on the diagonal to give fourteen 3in triangles (you will have one spare)
- Eight 1½ x 3in strips
- Twenty-four 1½ x 8in strips
- Enough 1½ x 5½in strips to fill the braid foundation rectangles (see Braid units)

Foundation fabric

- Four 6½in squares
- One 6½ x 15½in rectangle
- Two 6½ x 24½in rectangles
- Two 6½ x 33½in rectangles
- Two 6½ x 42½in rectangles
- Two 6½ x 51½in rectangles
- Two 6½ x 60½in rectangles
- Two 6½ x 69½in rectangles

Binding fabric

- Eight 2½in wide strips across the width of the fabric

Centre block

1 Take a 6½in foundation square. Right side up, place a 1½ x 8in scrappy strip across the square from corner to corner on the diagonal. Take a second 1½ x 8in scrappy strip and place it right side down on top of the first strip. Pin in place and sew along one long edge. Open the second strip out and press.

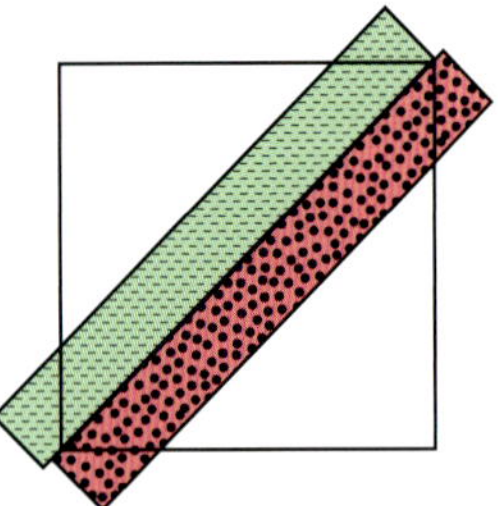

2 Carry on adding 1½ x 8in scrappy strips in the same manner, working both sides of the first strip, until you have approximately 1½in of foundation showing at opposite corners of the foundation square.

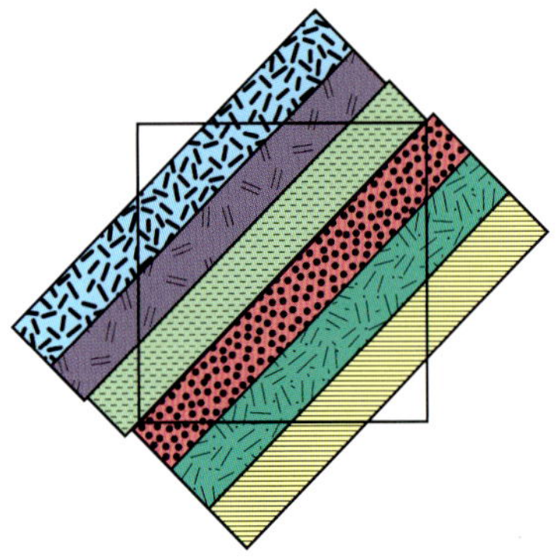

KISS: If using a removable foundation be sure to shorten the stitch length when sewing your strips in place, which will ensure the stitching doesn't come undone when removing the foundation paper.

3 Take a 1½ x 3in scrappy strip and place it right sides together with the outer rectangle at one corner of the foundation square, positioning it centrally along the length of the 1½ x 8in strip. Sew in place, flip the short strip open and press. Take a second 1½ x 3in scrappy strip and repeat for the other corner of the foundation square.

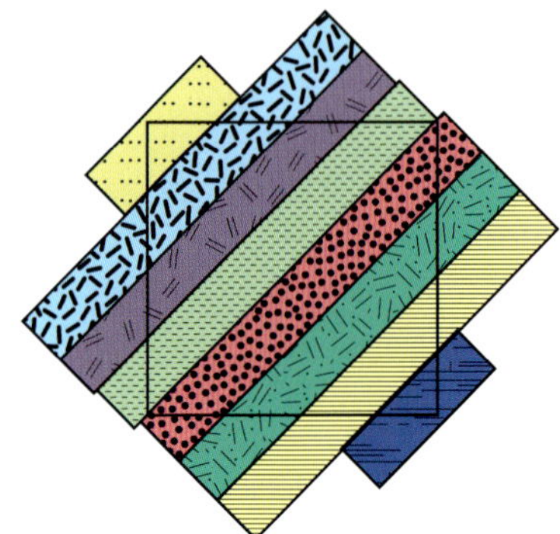

4 Trim the edges of the scrappy strips so they are level with the edges of the foundation square. This completes a quarter centre block.

5 Repeat Steps 1–4 to make a total of four quarter centre blocks.

6 Arrange the quarter centre blocks into two rows of two, making sure the short corner strips are at the centre and the outer corners of the full block (refer to the flat shot). Sew into rows and then sew the rows together. This completes the centre block, which should measure 12½in square.

Braid units

7 Take the 6½ x 15½in foundation rectangle. Matching up the raw edges, place a 3in scrappy triangle centrally at one short end (the bottom) of the foundation rectangle.

8 Right side down and matching up the raw edges, place a 1½ x 5½in scrappy strip down one side of the triangle.

9 Sew the strip in place, flip open and press.

10 Following Steps 8 and 9, add a 1½ x 5½in scrappy strip to the other side of the triangle.

11 Continue in the same manner as described in Steps 8–10, going back and forth between sides, until a tip of a strip touches the outer top edge of the foundation.

12 Take a 3½in background triangle and, matching up the raw edges, place it right side down on the strip at one top corner of the foundation.

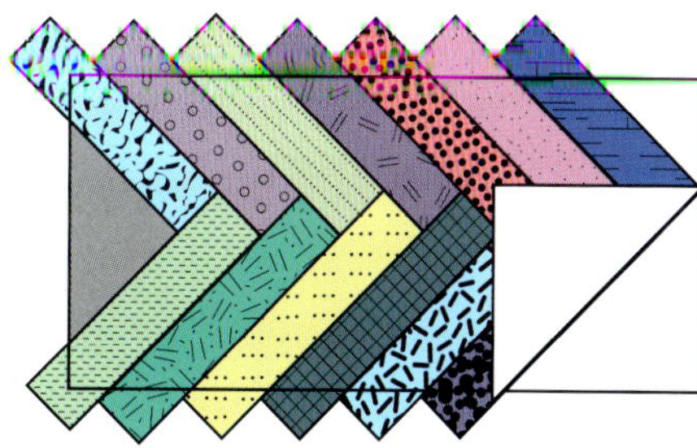

13 Sew the triangle in place, flip open and press.

14 Repeat Steps 12 and 13 to add a 3½in background triangle to the other top corner of the foundation.

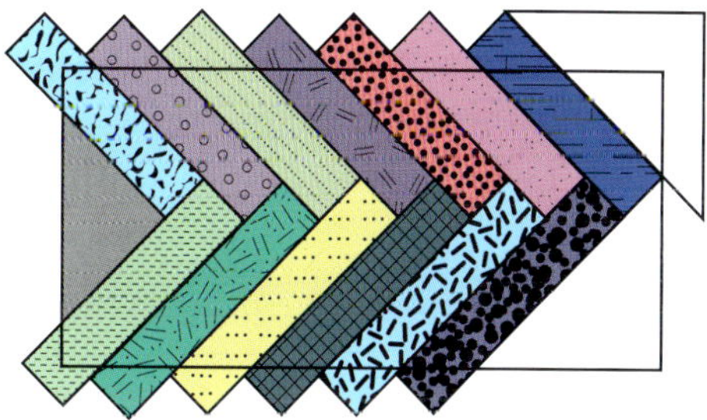

15 Trim the edges of the scrappy strips and background triangles so they are level with the edges of the foundation rectangle.

16 Repeat Steps 7–15 with the remaining foundation rectangles to make a total of thirteen braid units (see Cutting instructions for braid unit sizes).

Quilt assembly

Follow the layout diagram when constructing the quilt top. Note the orientations of the braid units.

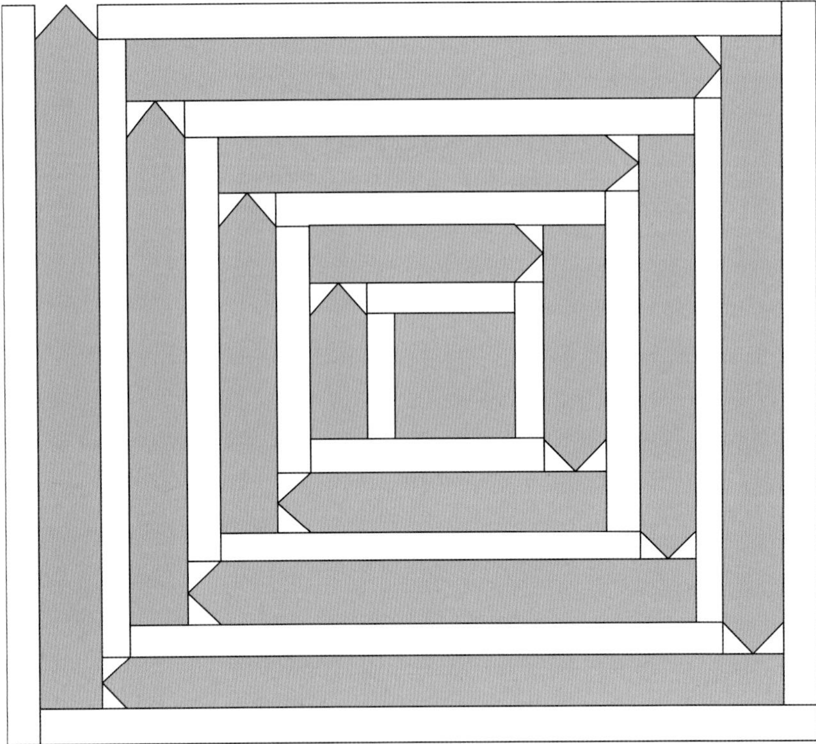

17 Sew the 3½ x 12½in background rectangle to the left-hand side of the centre block.

18 Sew a 3½ x 15½in background rectangle to the top of this unit. Sew the remaining 3½ x 15½in background rectangle to the right-hand side of this unit.

19 Sew a 6½ x 15½in braid unit to the left-hand side of the quilt.

20 Sew a 3½ x 24½in background rectangle to the bottom of the quilt.

21 Sew a 6½ x 24½in braid unit to the top of the quilt.

22 Sew a 3½ x 24½in background rectangle to the left-hand side of the quilt.

23 Sew a 6½ x 24½in braid unit to the right-hand side of the quilt.

24 Sew a 3½ x 33½in background rectangle to the top of the quilt.

25 Sew a 6½ x 33½in braid unit to the bottom of the quilt.

26 Sew a 3½ x 33½in background rectangle to the right-hand side of the quilt.

27 Sew a 6½ x 33½in braid unit to the left-hand side of the quilt.

28 Sew a 3½ x 42½in background rectangle to the bottom of the quilt.

29 Sew a 6½ x 42½in braid unit to the top of the quilt.

30 Sew a 3½ x 42½in background rectangle to the left-hand side of the quilt.

31 Sew a 6½ x 42½in braid unit to the right-hand side of the quilt.

32 Sew a 3½ x 51½in background rectangle to the top of the quilt.

33 Sew a 6½ x 51½in braid unit to the bottom of the quilt.

34 Sew a 3½ x 51½in background rectangle to the right-hand side of the quilt.

35 Sew a 6½ x 51½in braid unit to the left-hand side of the quilt.

36 Sew a 3½ x 60½in background rectangle to the bottom of the quilt.

37 Sew a 6½ x 60½in braid unit to the top of the quilt.

38 Sew a 3½ x 60½in background rectangle to the left-hand side of the quilt.

39 Sew a 6½ x 60½in braid unit to the right-hand side of the quilt.

40 Sew a 3½ x 69½in background rectangle to the top of the quilt.

41 Sew a 6½ x 69½in braid unit to the bottom of the quilt.

42 Sew a 3½ x 69½in background rectangle to the right-hand side of the quilt.

43 Sew a 6½ x 69½in braid unit to the left-hand side of the quilt.

44 Sew a 3½ x 78½in background rectangle to the bottom of the quilt.

45 Sew a 3½ x 72½in background rectangle to the left-hand side of the quilt. This completes your quilt top

Quilting and finishing

46 Make a quilt sandwich of the quilt top, the wadding (batting) and the backing fabric (see General Techniques, Making a quilt sandwich).

47 Quilt as desired. My quilt was quilted with feathers in the background fabric areas and echoing straight lines ¼in in from the seams in the braid units (see General Techniques, Quilting).

48 Square-up and bind to finish (see General Techniques, Squaring-up your quilt and Binding).

Enjoy your quilt.

ABUNDANCE

I love on-point quilts. Here, scrappy plus blocks are put on-point turning them into x's and multiplying the fun in this throw-size quilt.

Approximate size: 68 x 57in (173 x 145cm)

MATERIALS

- 3¼yds (3m) of background fabric
- Scrappy strips, at least 2½in wide by 10–20in long, totalling approximately 2yds (1.8m)
- 76 x 65in (193 x 165cm) of backing fabric
- ⅝yd (60cm) of binding fabric
- 76 x 65in (193 x 165cm) of wadding (batting)

KISS: If cutting your background fabric on the AccuQuilt cutting machine, cut five 7½in wide strips across the width of the fabric and place up to three strips at a time on the 2½in strip cutter die (die #50056) for a total of fifteen 2½in wide width-of-fabric strips.

Cutting instructions

ACCUQUILT GO! 50056

Background fabric

- Fourteen 2½in wide strips across the width of the fabric (for plus blocks) – you will need to subcut these to fit your 2½in wide scrappy strips (see Plus blocks). If using an AccuQuilt cutting machine, use die #50056 and see the KISS below
- One hundred and eighteen 2½ x 6½in rectangles (sashing rectangles)
- Twenty-two 2½in squares
- Five 9¼in squares for setting triangles
- Two 5⅛in squares for corner triangles

Scrappy strips

- 2½in wide strips by 10–20in long (for plus blocks) – if 10in long, you need approximately sixty-four strips; if 20in long, you need approximately thirty-two strips
- Forty-nine 2½in squares (for sashing rows)

Binding

- Seven 2½in wide strips across the width of the fabric

Plus blocks

1 Take three 2½in wide scrappy strips and join them on their long edges. Press each seam towards the outer strip. Subcut into 2½in wide segments.

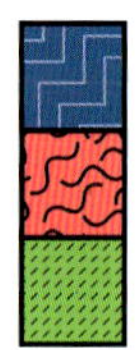

2 Repeat Step 1 until you have fifty scrappy strip-set segments.

3 Take one 2½in wide scrappy strip and two 2½in wide background strips and join on their long edges with the scrappy strip between the background strips. Press each seam towards the centre of the strip set. Subcut into 2½in wide segments.

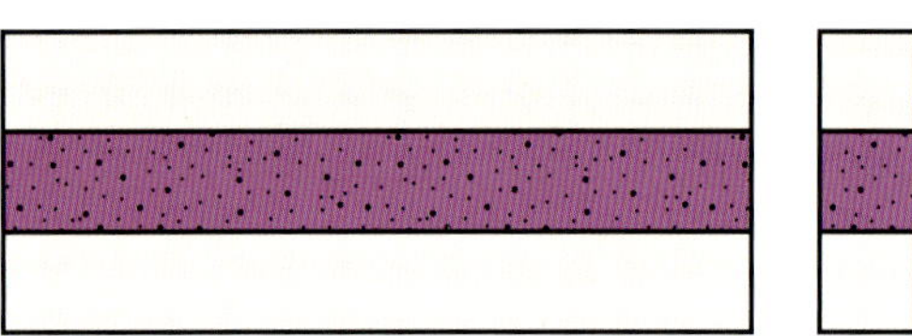

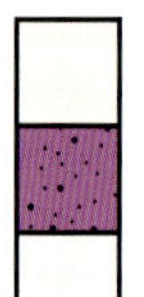

4 Repeat Step 3 until you have one hundred background/scrappy/background strip-set segments.

5 Take two background/scrappy/background strip-set segments and sew a scrappy strip-set segment between them. This completes one plus block, which should measure 6½in square.

6 Repeat Step 5 to make a total of fifty plus blocks.

Quilt assembly

Follow the layout diagram when constructing the quilt top.

STRIP PROJECTS

7 Take the 9¼in setting-triangle squares and cut each twice on the diagonal to give twenty setting triangles (you will have two spare).

8 Take the 5⅛in corner-triangle squares and cut each once on the diagonal to give four corner triangles.

9 Refer to the flat shot and follow On-point settings (see General Techniques, Piecing) – note that rows start at the top left corner. Arrange the plus blocks into ten diagonal rows with a 2½ x 6½in sashing strip rectangle between each block and at each end – rows 1 and 10 will just have a sashing strip rectangle either side of a single block. Sew each row together with a setting triangle at each end of rows 1–4 and rows 7–10, a setting triangle at the left-hand edge only of row 5 and a setting triangle at the right-hand edge only of row 6.

10 Between the block rows, arrange the remaining 2½ x 6½in sashing strip rectangles and 2½in scrappy squares into diagonal rows. Note that a sashing strip rectangle will be between blocks of subsequent block rows and the scrappy squares will be between the sashing strips. Sew each row together with a 2½in background square at each end of each row. Note that the 2½in background squares will be trimmed to create triangles in Step 12.

11 Join the block rows and sashing rows, adding the corner triangles last.

12 Trim so you have straight edges. Your quilt top is now complete.

KISS: If you wish, instead of a single-fabric binding, you could make a scrappy binding (see General Techniques, Binding).

Quilting and finishing

13 Make a quilt sandwich of the quilt top, the wadding (batting) and the backing fabric (see General Techniques, Making a quilt sandwich).

14 Quilt as desired. My quilt was quilted with an allover loopy meandering flower motif (see General Techniques, Quilting).

15 Square-up and bind to finish (see General Techniques, Squaring-up your quilt and Binding).

Enjoy your quilt.

STREAK OF LIGHTNING

The quintessential rail fence block is classic. Making one rail from strip sets and then cutting the rails so they have varying angles draws on tradition while giving a striking contemporary vibe.

Approximate size: 79 x 63in (200 x 160cm)

MATERIALS

- 3yds (2.8m) low-volume background fabrics
- Scrappy strips and strings, totalling approximately 3½yds (3.2m) – I used bold blues, browns, greens and reds
- 87 x 71in (220 x 180cm) of backing fabric
- ⅝yd (60cm) of binding fabric
- 87 x 71in (220 x 180cm) of wadding (batting)

Cutting instructions

ACCUQUILT GO!
55000

Background fabrics

- Ninety 6½in squares or ninety AccuQuilt die #55000

Scrappy strips

- Sew strips into 7in wide strip sets. Cut into ninety 6½in squares or ninety AccuQuilt die #55000

Binding fabric

- Eight 2½in wide strips across the width of the fabric

KISS: For details about how to make strip sets see Creating the Basics, Making a strip/string set. If you use long and short strings in each strip set you can rearrange them, which enables you to create greater variety without having to make lots of different strip sets. When a string runs out, simply remove it and add it to a longer strip in the strip set or toss it into your crumb-fabric bin for future use.

Streak of lightning blocks

1 Place a 6½in background square right side up and then place a 6½in strip-set square on top, also right side up and with the strips running vertically. Cut a diagonal line from side edge to side edge, leaving at least 1in above and below the cut on each side.

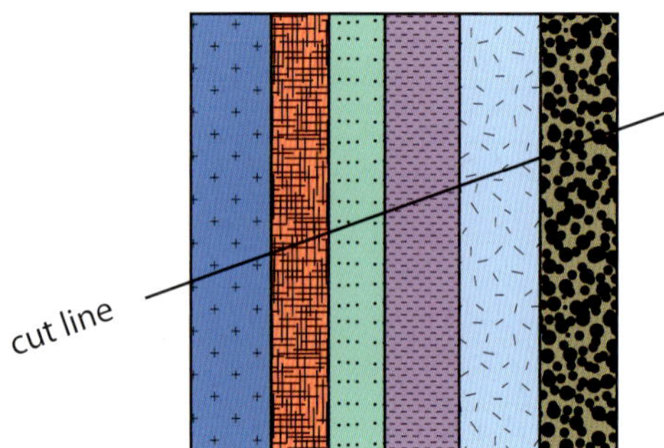

2 Sew the top strip-set section to the bottom background section. Square-up to 5¾in square.

3 Sew the bottom strip-set section to the top background section. Square-up to 5¾in square.

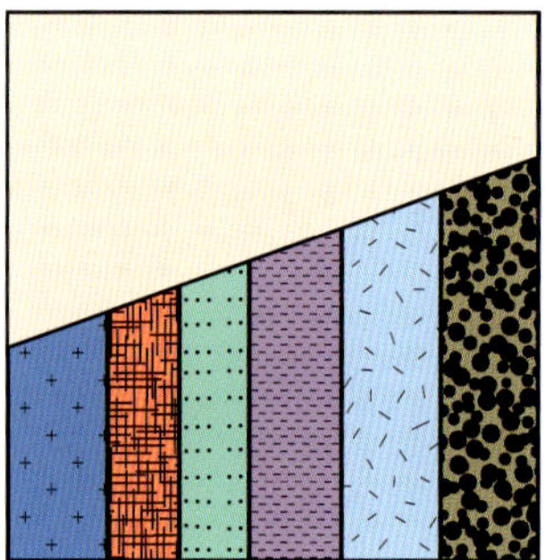

4 Repeat Steps 1–3 with the remaining 6½in background and strip-set squares to make a total of one hundred and eighty streak of lightning blocks.

Quilt assembly

5 Arrange the blocks into fifteen rows of twelve blocks each. On odd-numbered rows, start with a background section at the top of the block and arrange every other block in the same orientation, then orientate the blocks in between them with the background section on the left-hand side of the block. On even-numbered rows, start with a background section on the left-hand side of the block and arrange every other block in the same orientation, then orientate the blocks in between them with the background section at the top of the block. Refer to the flat shot.

6 Sew the blocks into rows and then join the rows. This completes your quilt top.

Quilting and finishing

7 Make a quilt sandwich of the quilt top, the wadding (batting) and the backing fabric (see General Techniques, Making a quilt sandwich).

8 Quilt as desired. My quilt was quilted with an allover pattern made up of squares and circles (see General Techniques, Quilting).

9 Square-up and bind to finish (see General Techniques, Squaring-up your quilt and Binding).

Enjoy your quilt.

ESCAPE

Designed for my new king-sized bed, Escape gets outside the box with bold quarter square Log Cabins of various shades of grey and vibrant prints arranged into partial squares, so you'll never feel boxed in.

Approximate size: 113 x 95in (287 x 241cm)

MATERIALS

- 4⅝yds (4.3m) of dark grey fabric (includes binding)
- 1¼yds (1.2m) of medium grey fabric
- 1⅝yds (1.5m) of light grey fabric
- Various bright prints, totalling approximately 5½yds (5m) – see Cutting instructions
- 121 x 103in (307 x 261cm) of backing fabric
- 121 x 103in (307 x 261cm) of wadding (batting)

KISS: For your bright prints, choose bold and vibrant colours and designs that will contrast with the subdued grey fabrics, then they will really zing!

Cutting instructions

Dark grey fabric

- Ninety-nine 3in squares
- One hundred and seventy-eight 1½ x 9½in rectangles (sashing strips)
- Five 2½in wide strips across the width of the fabric. Sew end to end and then subcut into two 2½ x 95½in strips (top and bottom borders)
- Six 3½in wide strips across the width of the fabric. Sew end to end and then subcut into two 3½ x 109½in strips (side borders)
- Eleven 2½in wide strips across the width of the fabric (binding)

Medium grey fabric

- Ninety-nine 1½ x 4½in rectangles
- Ninety-nine 1½ x 5½in rectangles

Light grey fabric

- Ninety-nine 1½ x 7in rectangles
- Ninety-nine 1½ x 8in rectangles

Various bright prints

- Ninety-nine 2 x 3in rectangles and ninety-nine corresponding 2 x 4½in rectangles
- Ninety-nine 2 x 5½in rectangles and ninety-nine corresponding 2 x 7in rectangles
- Ninety-nine 2 x 8in rectangles and ninety-nine corresponding 2 x 9½in rectangles
- Eighty 1½in squares

Quarter Log Cabin blocks

1 Take a 3in dark grey square, and a bright print 2 x 3in rectangle and its corresponding 2 x 4½in rectangle. Sew the shorter rectangle to the top of the square and then sew the longer rectangle to the right-hand side.

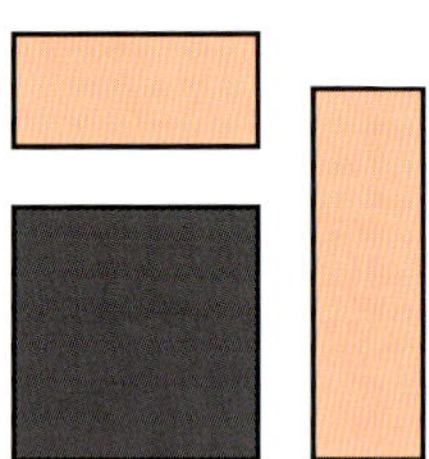

2 Sew a 1½ x 4½in medium grey rectangle to the top of the unit made in Step 1, and then sew a 1½ x 5½in medium grey rectangle to the right-hand side.

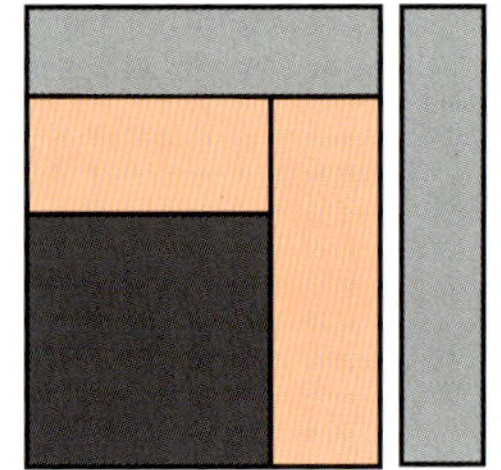

3 Take a bright print 2 x 5½in rectangle and its corresponding 2 x 7in rectangle. Sew the shorter rectangle to the top of the unit made in Step 2 and then sew the longer rectangle to the right-hand side.

4 Sew a 1½ x 7in light grey rectangle to the top of the unit made in Step 3, and then sew a 1½ x 8in light grey rectangle to the right-hand side.

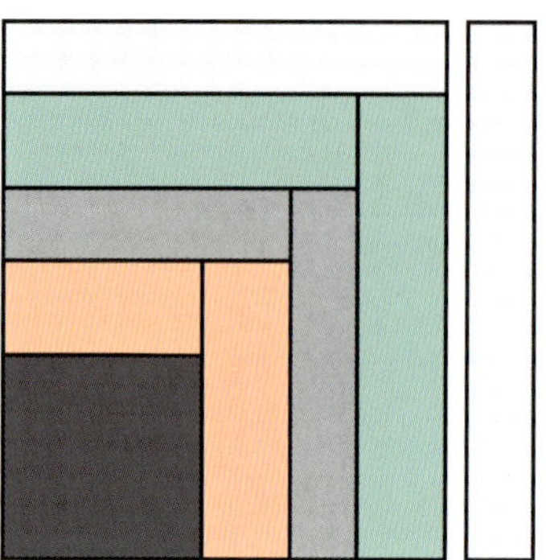

5 Take a bright print 2 x 8in rectangle and its corresponding 2 x 9½in rectangle. Sew the shorter rectangle to the top of the unit made in Step 4 and then sew the longer rectangle to the right-hand side. This completes one Quarter Log Cabin block, which should measure 9½in square.

6 Repeat Steps 1–5 to make a total of ninety-nine Quarter Log Cabin blocks.

Quilt assembly

Follow the layout diagram when constructing the quilt top.

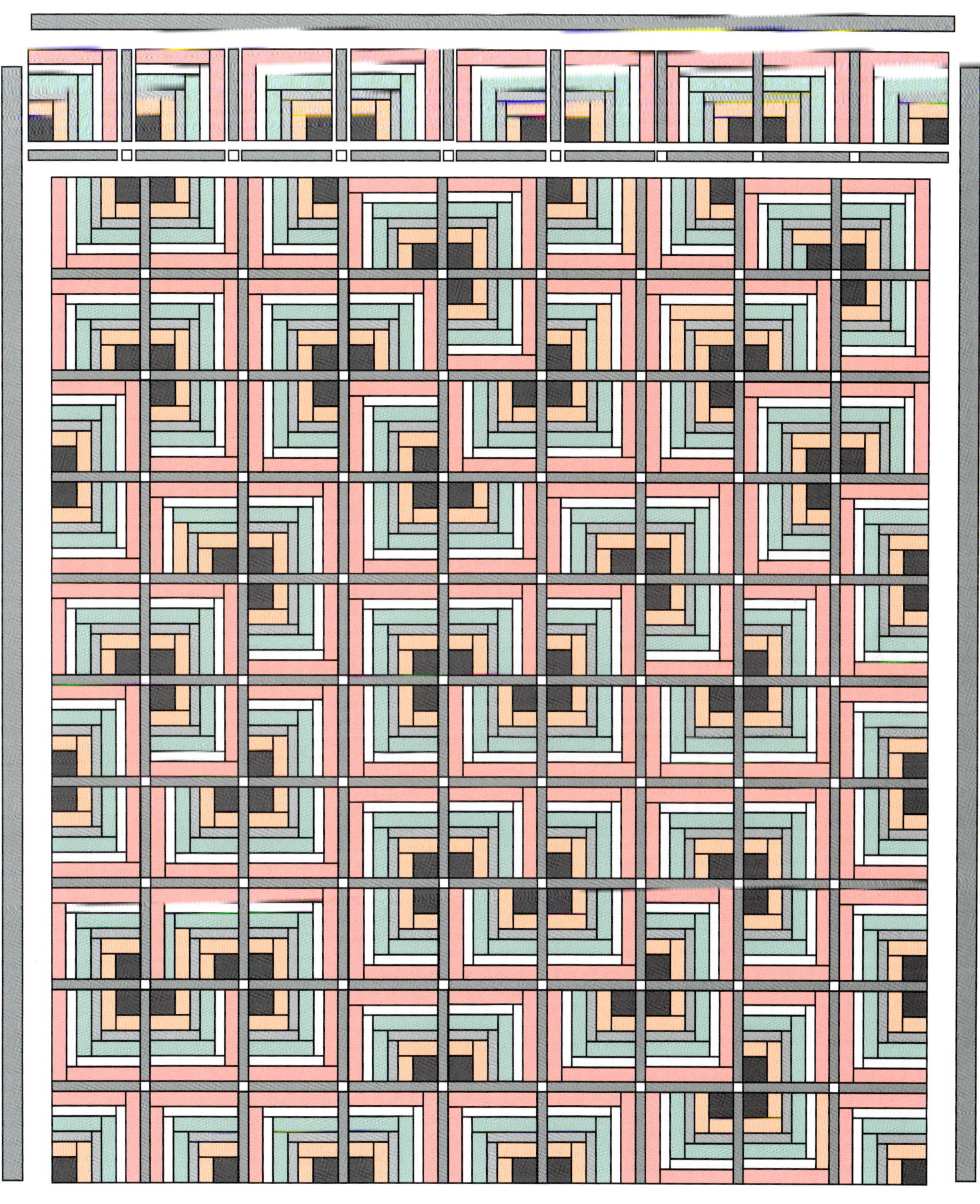

STRIP PROJECTS

7 Arrange your Quarter Log Cabin blocks into eleven rows of nine blocks each with a 1½ x 9½in dark grey sashing strip rectangle between each block. Note the orientations of the Quarter Log Cabin blocks.

8 Sew the blocks and rectangles into rows.

9 Between each block row, arrange nine 1½ x 9½in dark grey sashing strip rectangles with a 1½in bright print square between each rectangle. You will have ten sashing strip rows in total.

10 Sew the sashing strip rows together. Then join the block and sashing strip rows to complete the quilt centre.

11 Sew a 3½ x109½in dark grey border strip to each side of the quilt centre.

12 Sew a 2½ x 95½in dark grey border strip to the top and bottom of the quilt centre. This completes your quilt top.

Quilting and finishing

13 Make a quilt sandwich of the quilt top, the wadding (batting) and the backing fabric (see General Techniques, Making a quilt sandwich).

14 Quilt as desired. My quilt was quilted with a large allover floral motif (see General Techniques, Quilting).

15 Square-up and bind to finish (see General Techniques, Squaring-up your quilt and Binding).

Enjoy your quilt.

KISS: When choosing the bright prints for your blocks keep in mind how value and contrast works. As dark grey is used in the centre, dark value prints in the centre will blend in and not pop, so use medium or light value prints here. The opposite is true with the outer part of the block where light grey is used, that is, light value prints will blend in, so use medium and dark value prints here.

COMBINATION PROJECTS

Let all your scraps come out to play while you create statement-worthy projects. Combine strips and crumbs into pillows and quilts for snuggling up with.

POWERPUFF TRIO

Featuring a dynamic pinwheel made from crumb fabric, a sampler of strip blocks, and a striking square-in-a-square design blending strips and crumbs, this trio of pillows is sure to make a bold statement.

Approximate size: each pillow is 16in (40cm) square

MATERIALS

- Various fabrics – see each block's instructions for details

Cutting instructions

Various fabrics

- See each block's instructions for details

KISS: Try going bold with your background fabric. When doing this pull prints that contrast with the background, remembering how value works. If you want things to blend, use low contrast prints, but if you want them to pop then go for high contrast.

Crumb pillow top

MATERIALS

- One 9¼in square of background fabric
- Two 15in made crumb-fabric squares – see Creating the Basics, Making crumb fabric

Cutting instructions

BACKGROUND FABRIC

- Cut the 9¼in square twice on the diagonal to give four triangles

CRUMB FABRIC

- From each 15in square cut two 6¼ x 12¼in rectangles (four in total)

Sewing

1 Take one background triangle and one crumb rectangle. Right sides together, place triangle on top of rectangle as shown and sew them together on the line indicated.

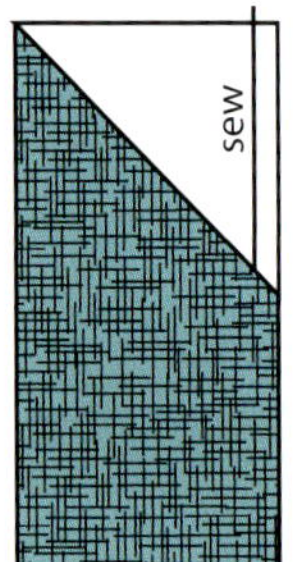

2 Flip the triangle and press the seam towards the background fabric.

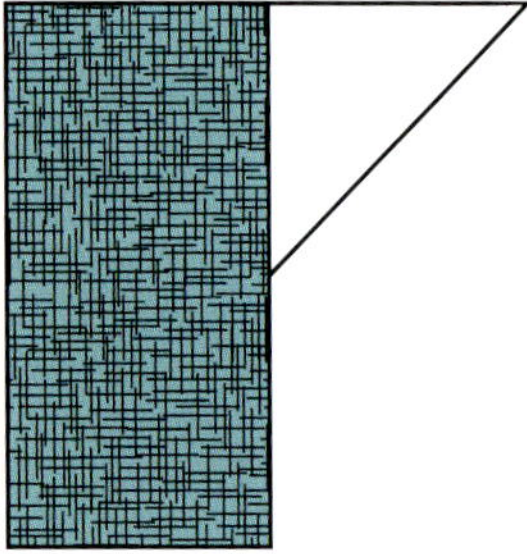

3 Repeat Steps 1 and 2 with the remaining background triangles and crumb rectangles to make a total of four triangle/rectangle units.

4 Arrange the triangle/rectangle units as shown.

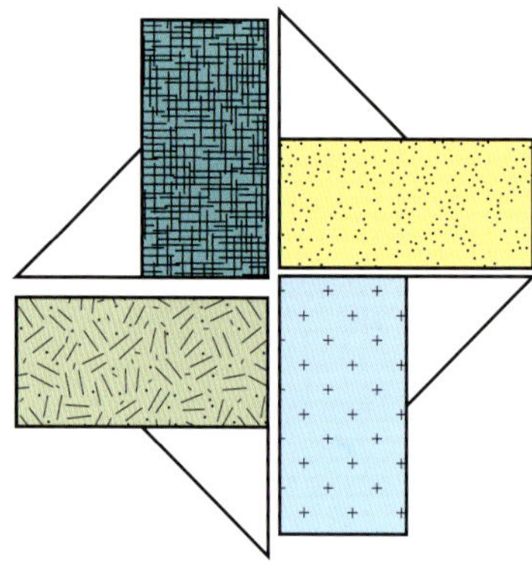

5 Sew the units into pairs and then join the pairs. Keeping the centre point of pillow top centred, square-up to 16½in square. This completes the Crumb pillow top. Set aside.

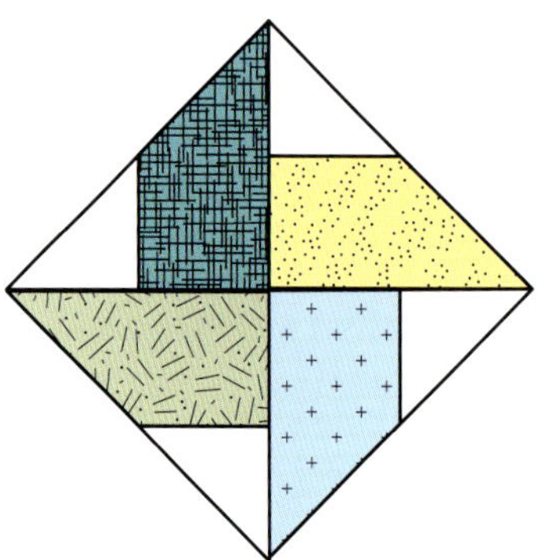

Strip sampler pillow top

MATERIALS

- ¼yd (25cm) of background fabric
- Scrappy strips, at least 1½in wide in a variety of lengths, totalling approximately ⅛yd (15cm) for the Log Cabin section (see Cutting instructions)
- Four 2½ x 4½in scrappy rectangles for the flying geese section
- Scrappy strips and strings of various widths, but at least 10in long, totalling approximately ⅛yd (15cm) for the large and small strip-set sections

Cutting instructions

BACKGROUND FABRIC

- One 1 x 7½in rectangle
- One 1 x 8½in rectangle
- Two 1½ x 4½in rectangles
- Four 1½ x 6½in rectangles
- One 1½ x 7½in rectangle
- One 1½ x 8in rectangle
- Two 1½ x 16½in rectangles
- Eight 2½in squares

SCRAPPY 1½IN WIDE STRIPS

- Two 1½in squares
- Two 1½ x 2½in rectangles
- Two 1½ x 3½in rectangles
- Two 1½ x 4½in rectangles
- Two 1½ x 5½in rectangles
- Two 1½ x 6½in rectangles

Sewing

6 Using your strips that are at least 10in long, create a strip set that is at least 16in high (see Creating the Basics, Making a strip/string set).

7 From the strip set made in Step 6, cut:

- One 14½ x 6½in strip-set rectangle
- One 6½ x 2½in strip-set rectangle

KISS: **When cutting the strip-set rectangles, be mindful that seams need to be at least ½in in from the top and bottom edges. This ensures the strips show in the finished piece and there is not excessive bulk in the seams.**

8 Sew a 1½ x 6½in background rectangle to each 6½in edge of the 14½ x 6½in strip-set rectangle. Then sew a 1½ x 16½in background rectangle to each long (16½in) edge. This completes the large strip-set section. Set aside.

9 Sew a 1½ x 6½in background rectangle to each 6½in edge of the 6½ x 2½in strip-set rectangle. Then sew a 1½ x 4½in background rectangle to each short (4½in) edge. This completes the small strip-set section. Set aside.

10 Sew the two 1½in scrappy squares together.

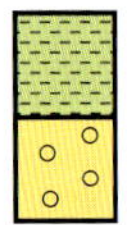

11 Sew a 1½ x 2½in scrappy rectangle to the left-hand side of the unit made in Step 10.

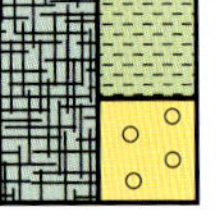

COMBINATION PROJECTS

12 Sew the remaining 1½ x 2½in scrappy rectangle to the bottom of the unit made in Step 11.

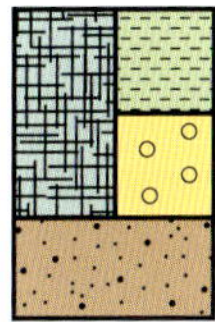

13 Sew a 1½ x 3½in scrappy rectangle to the right-hand side of the unit made in Step 12. Then sew the remaining 1½ x 3½in scrappy rectangle to the top of the unit.

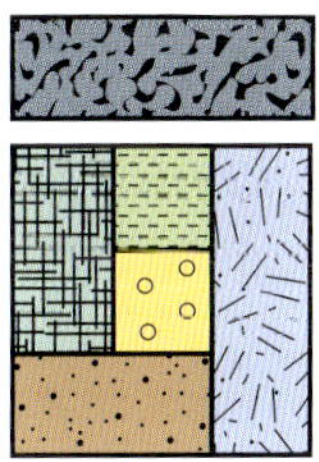

14 Sew a 1½ x 4½in scrappy rectangle to the left-hand side of the unit made in Step 13. Then sew the remaining 1½ x 4½in scrappy rectangle to the bottom of the unit.

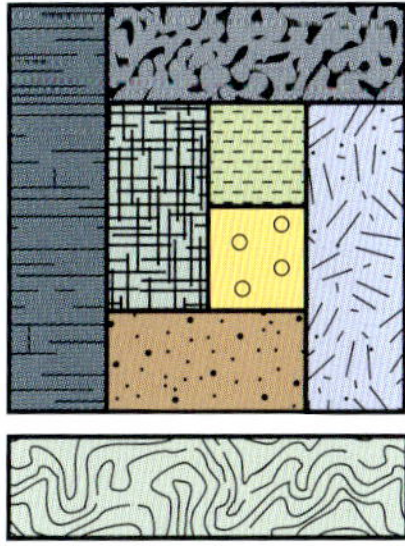

15 Sew a 1½ x 5½in scrappy rectangle to the right-hand side of the unit made in Step 14. Then sew the remaining 1½ x 5½in scrappy rectangle to the top of the unit.

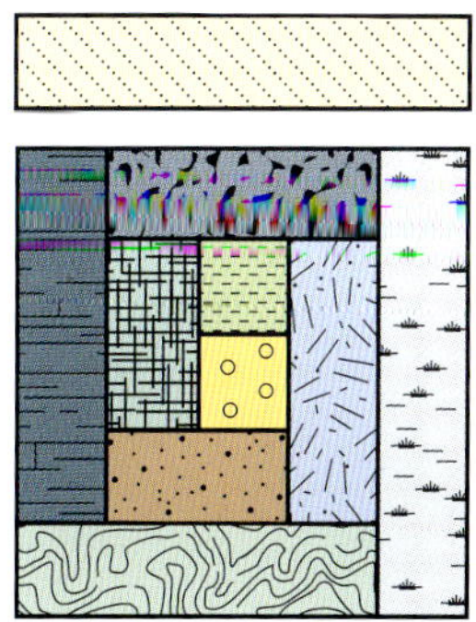

16 Sew a 1½ x 6½in scrappy rectangle to the left-hand side of the unit made in Step 15. Then sew the remaining 1½ x 6½in scrappy rectangle to the bottom of the unit.

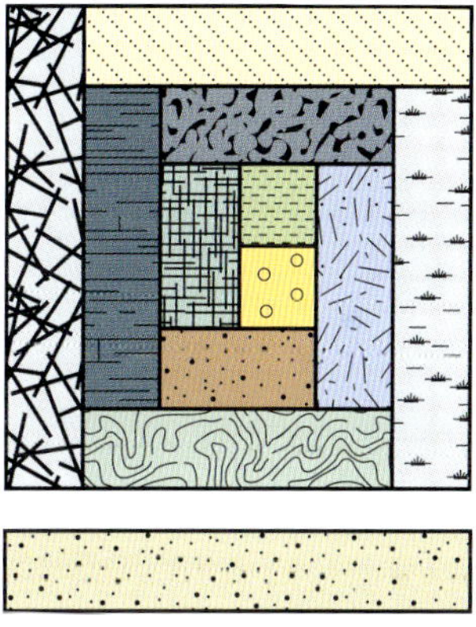

17 Sew the 1½ x 7½in background rectangle to the right-hand side of unit made in Step 16, then add the 1 x 7½in background rectangle to the top edge.

18 Sew the 1½ x 8in background rectangle to the left-hand side of the unit made in Step 17, then add the 1 x 8½in rectangle to the bottom edge. This completes the Log Cabin section. Set aside.

19 Take two 2½in background squares and one 2½ x 4½in scrappy rectangle. On the wrong side of each square mark a diagonal line from corner to corner.

20 Working on one corner at a time, right sides together, place a square on top of one corner, with the diagonal line running from the bottom corner to the top edge. Stitch on the marked line.

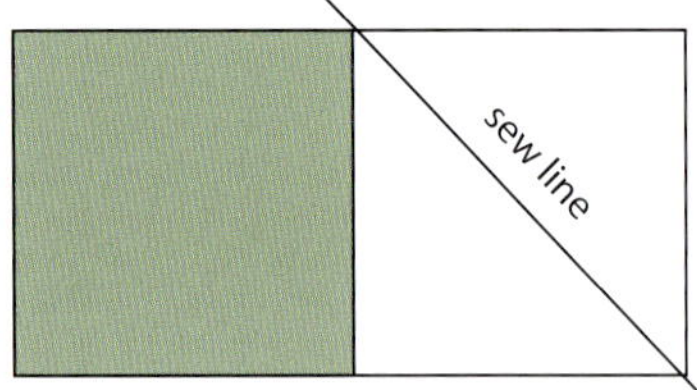

21 Trim ¼in beyond the stitched line then flip the corner open and press.

22 Repeat Steps 20 and 21 for the other corner to complete one flying goose unit.

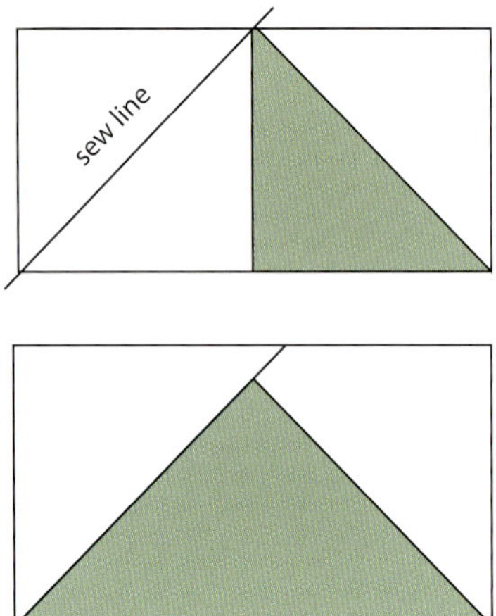

23 Repeat Steps 19–22 with the remaining 2½in background squares and 2½ x 4½in scrappy rectangles to make a total of four flying geese units.

24 With the geese flying in the same direction, join the four flying geese into a strip.

25 Referring to the finished project photo, with the geese flying upwards, sew the Log Cabin section to the left-hand side of the flying geese strip and the small strip-set section to the right-hand side.

26 Sew the large strip-set section to the top of the unit made in Step 25. This completes the Strip sampler pillow top. Set aside.

Combo pillow top

MATERIALS

- One 3½in wide strip of background fabric
- One 7in or larger made crumb-fabric square – see Creating the Basics, Making crumb fabric
- Scrappy strips of various widths, but at least 7–14in long, totalling approximately ⅜yd (40cm)
- Two 9in (23cm) squares of foundation fabric

Cutting instructions

BACKGROUND FABRIC

- Two 3½ x 6in rectangles
- Two 3½ x 11½in rectangles

CRUMB FABRIC

- One 6in square

KISS: I like to use a permanent foundation fabric – lightweight calico (muslin) is my go-to – as I don't have to rip it off later and it helps to keep the bias edges from stretching.

Sewing

27 Sew a 3½ x 6in background rectangle to two opposite sides of the 6in crumb square. Then sew the 3½ x 11½in background rectangles to the two remaining opposite sides. This completes the pillow centre. Set aside.

28 Take a 9in foundation square. Right side up, place a scrappy strip across the square from corner to corner on the diagonal. Pin or glue in place.

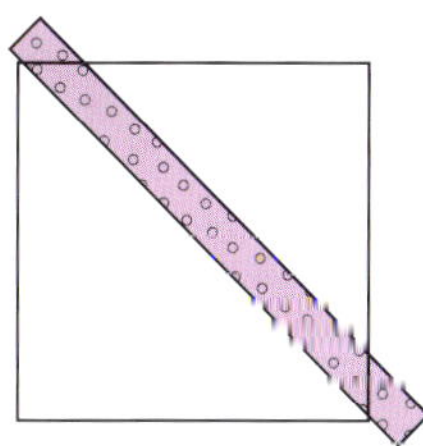

29 Take a second scrappy strip and place it right side down on top of the first strip, matching up the long raw edges on one side. Pin in place and sew along the long edges that match up. Open the second strip out and press.

30 Continue as in Step 29 to fill one half of the foundation.

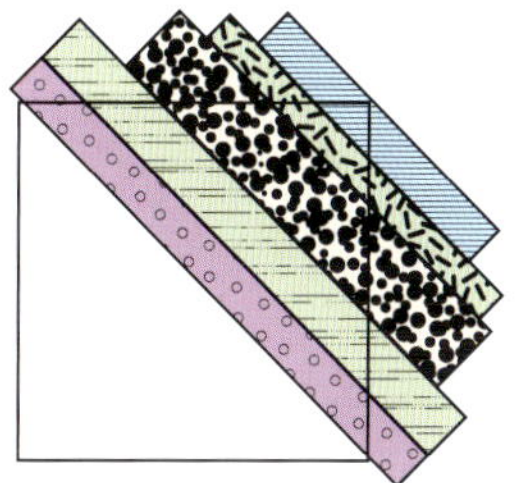

31 Trim the edges of the scrappy strips so they are level with the edges of the foundation square.

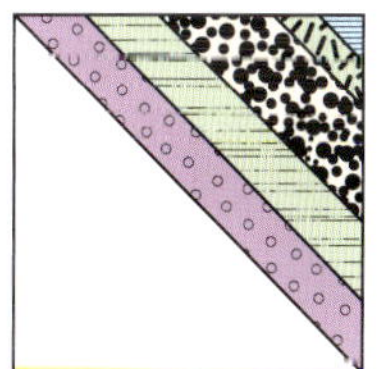

32 Repeat Steps 29 and 30 to fill the other half of the foundation.

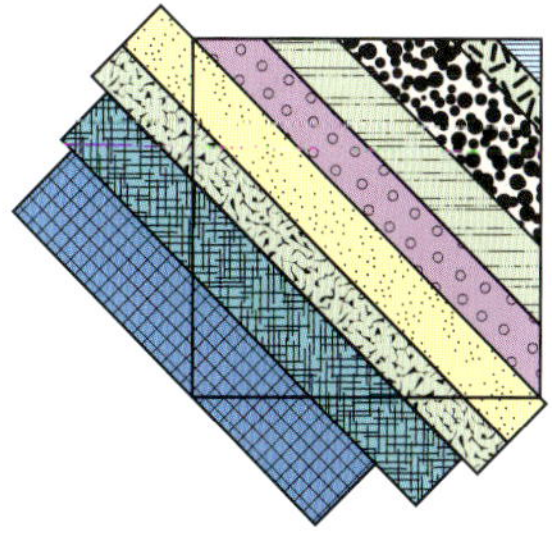

33 Trim the edges of the scrappy strips so they are level with the edges of the foundation square. Then cut the square once on the diagonal, with the cut running on the opposite diagonal to the strips.

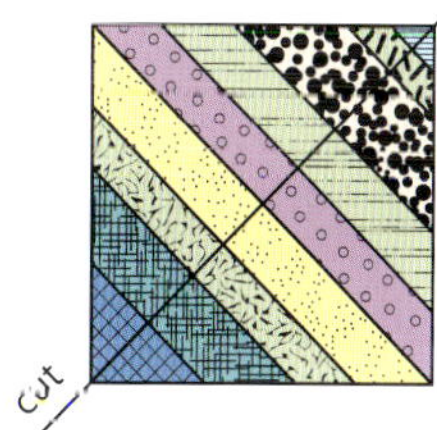

34 Repeat Steps 28–33 to make a total of four scrappy-strip triangles.

35 Sew a scrappy-strip triangle to two opposite sides of the pillow centre made in Step 27. Then sew the remaining scrappy-strip triangles to the two remaining opposite sides of the pillow centre.

36 Keeping the centre point of the pillow top centred, square-up to 16½in square. This completes the Combo pillow top. Set aside.

Completing the pillows

MATERIALS TO COMPLETE THE THREE PILLOWS

- Six 10½ x 16½in (27 x 42cm) backing rectangles (two for each pillow)
- Three 16in (40cm) square cushion pads (pillow forms)
- 1½yds (1.4m) of ½in (1.25cm) wide sew-in Velcro tape

Cutting instructions

VELCRO TAPE

- Four 12in long strips

Sewing

37 Take a pair of 10½ x 16½in backing rectangles. On one long edge of each rectangle, turn under ¼in to the wrong side and press. Then turn over 1in and press again.

38 Topstitch in place along the folded edge.

39 Take one pillow back piece and place it right side up. Take one 12in strip of Velcro tape and centre the hook side of the tape along the folded edge of the pillow back, approximately ⅛in down from the fold. Pin to secure and then stitch in place

40 Take the remaining pillow back piece and place it wrong side up. Centre the loop side of the Velcro tape along the folded edge, approximately ⅛in down from the fold. Pin to secure and then stitch in place.

41 Take one of your pillow tops and place it right side up. Right side down and matching up the raw edges, place the pillow back piece made in Step 40 (loop side of the tape) on top, with the Velcro edge running across the centre. In the same way, place the pillow back piece made in Step 39 (hook side of the tape) in place. The pillow back pieces should overlap and the Velcro hooks and loops should match up.

42 Pin all around to secure. Take extra care where the pillow back pieces overlap and make sure the Velcro pieces match up. If you wish, baste where the pillow back pieces overlap. Sew all around with a ¼in seam. For extra strength, you could sew a second row of stitching where the pillow back pieces overlap.

43 Trim the corners, taking care not to snip your stitching. Turn right side out through the overlapped edges. Insert a cushion pad (pillow form), plump up and then close the Velcro fastening.

44 Repeat Steps 37–43 for the two remaining pillows.

Enjoy your pillows.

FIREWORKS

I love fireworks, feeling the BOOM! Seeing the bright flashes against a dark sky. Now I can snuggle under a fireworks quilt while I enjoy the show.

Approximate size: 78 x 70in (198 x 178cm)

MATERIALS

- Enough grey and black made crumb fabric to cut one hundred and thirty-two Triangle templates, twelve Half-triangle templates and twelve Half-triangle reverse templates (if you wish, use some grey and black scraps for some single-fabric triangles and half-triangles, too)
- Enough grey and black made crumb fabric to cut ninety-six made crumb-fabric plus brights Triangle templates
- Enough grey and black scraps and strips to make the top and bottom borders – see Quilt assembly
- An assortment of 1½ x 20in bright fabric strips, totally approximately ¼yd (25cm) – see Made crumb-fabric plus brights strips Triangle templates
- 86 x 78in (218 x 198cm) of backing fabric
- ⅝yd (60cm) of binding fabric
- 86 x 78in (218 x 198cm) of wadding (batting)

Cutting instructions

Binding fabric

- Eight 2½in wide strips across the width of the fabric

KISS: If you wish, the 1½ x 20in bright fabric strips could be cut from fat quarters.

KISS: When cutting out your half-triangles (for the sides of the quilt), remember that twelve are Half-triangle templates and twelve are Half-triangle reverse templates. For the Half-triangle reverse templates, simply flip the Half-triangle template over before cutting out.

Made crumb-fabric only Triangle and Half-triangle templates

1 Make around sixty 8 x 16in crumb-fabric strips (see Creating the Basics, Making crumb fabric).

KISS: Your crumb fabric will lay flatter and be easier to work with if you make chunks of crumb fabric at least 16in square and then cut that into two strips. Simply straighten up the short ends and then join the pieces into a longer strip.

KISS: If you make crumb-fabric strips wider than required, you can play with cutting to reduce seams along the cut edges, which avoids excessive bulk in the seams when joining triangles.

2 From your crumb-fabric strip, cut as many Triangle templates as you can. Sew any unused strip to the next crumb-fabric strip on the short edge and then cut as many Triangle templates as you can from this new strip.

3 Continue working in this way until you have one hundred and thirty-two crumb Triangle templates. If required, make a few more crumb-fabric strips.

4 In the same manner as in Steps 2 and 3, cut twelve Half-triangle and twelve Half-triangle reverse crumb templates.

KISS: If the cut edge of a strip becomes distorted when you are cutting out templates, place the template so some strip extends beyond it and then cut along the edge of the template to restore the edge, and then continue cutting out template pieces.

Made crumb-fabric plus brights strips Triangle templates

5 Make around forty-five 4½ x 16in crumb-fabric strips (see Creating the Basics, Making crumb fabric). Sew a 1½in wide bright fabric strip to each long edge of each crumb strip to give 6½in wide strips.

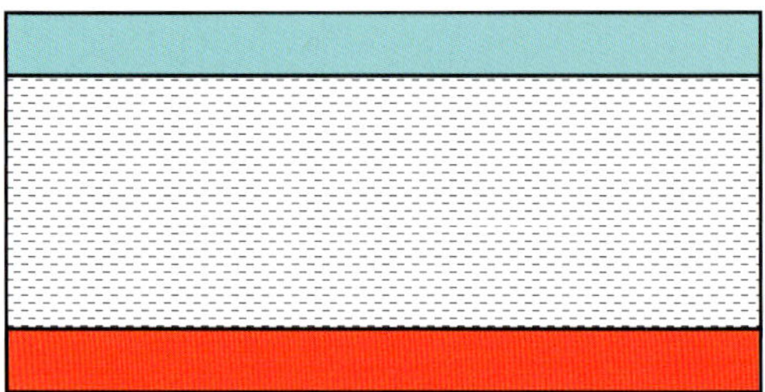

6 Cut as many Triangle templates as you can from one crumb plus brights strip.

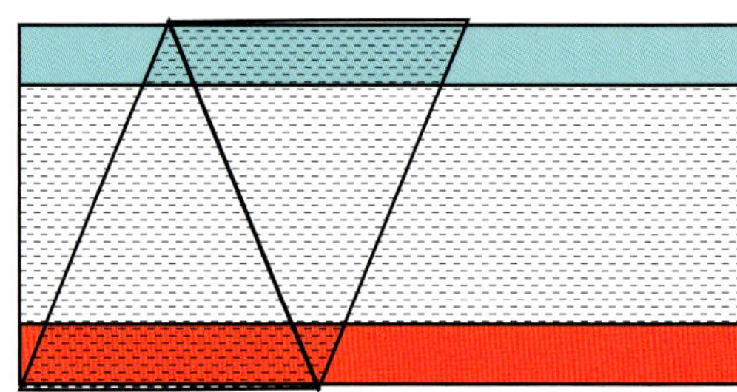

7 Sew any unused strip to the next crumb plus brights strip on the short edge and then cut as many Triangle templates as you can from this new strip.

8 Continue working in this way until you have ninety-six Triangle templates. If required, make a few more crumb plus brights strips.

Quilt assembly

Follow the layout diagram when constructing the quilt top.

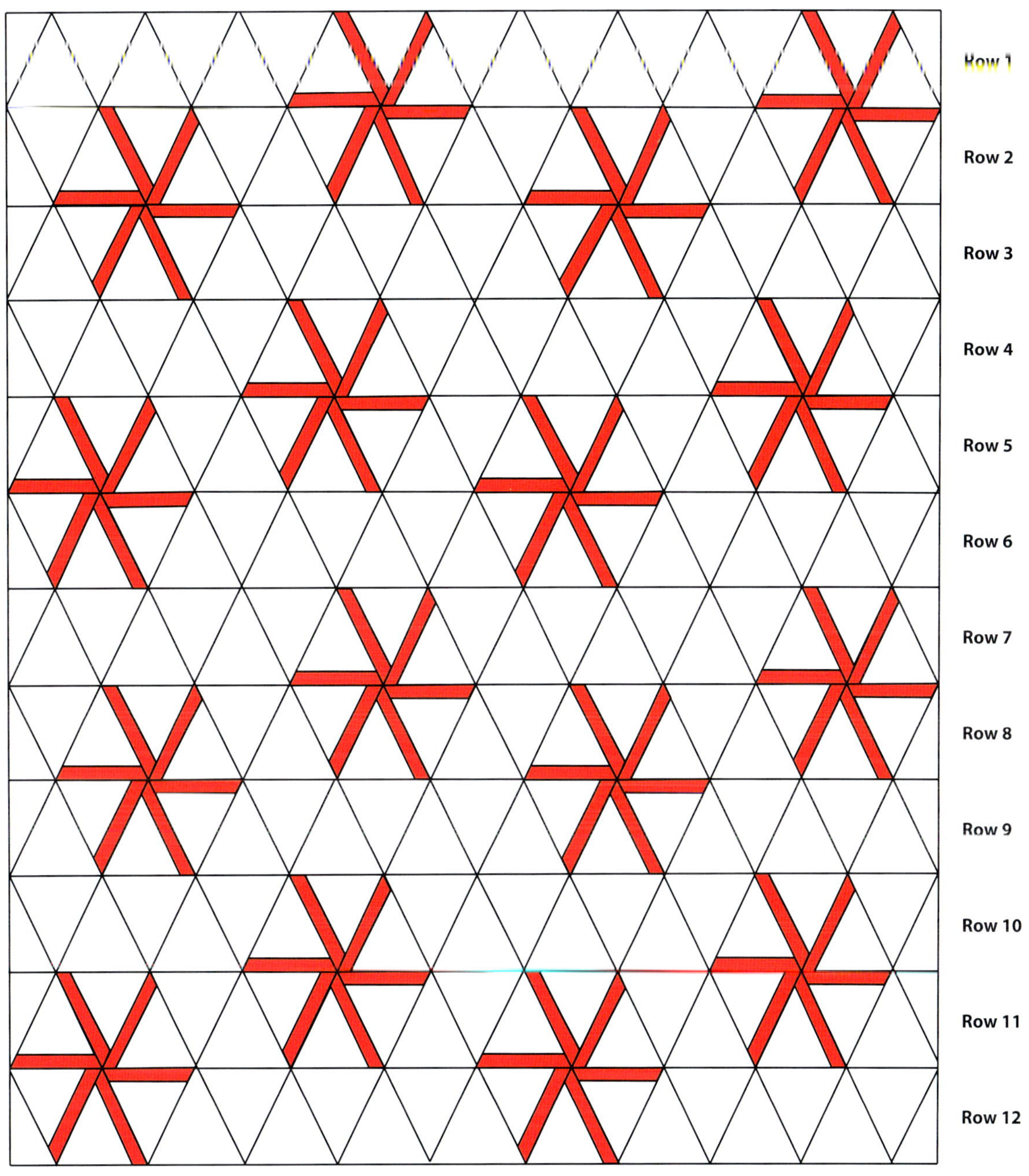

9 Arrange your crumb Triangles and crumb plus brights Triangles into twelve rows of nineteen triangles each. Note the placements and orientations of the crumb plus brights Triangles. You will need one crumb Half-triangle and one crumb Half-triangle reverse to complete the ends of each row.

10 To make the rows, working from left to right, place the first two triangles right sides together, matching up all the raw edges and with the second triangle on top. Sew down the right-hand edge. Open the triangles out and press. Continue to work along the row in the same manner. Add the half-triangles at either end last. As you are making the rows, on odd-numbered rows press the seams to the right, and on even-numbered rows press the seams to the left, then when the rows are joined the seam intersections will nestle together neatly.

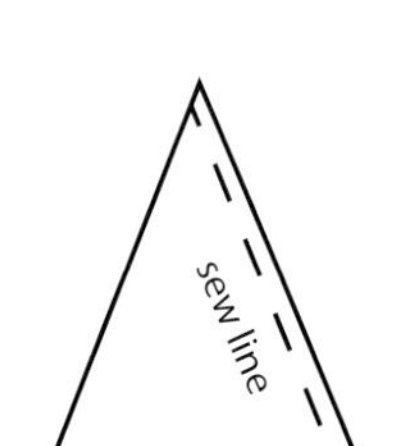

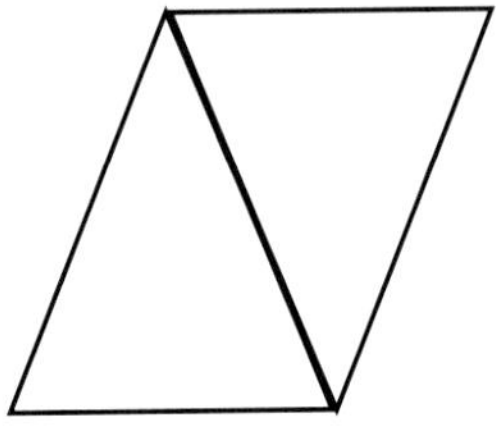

11 Join the rows to complete the quilt centre.

12 Use the grey and black scraps and strips to cut out squares and rectangles and to make small rail fence-style blocks. The units need to be 3½in high. Join the units to make two 3½in high x 70½in long border strips.

KISS: By adding a border of squares, rectangles and rail fence-style blocks at the top and bottom of your quilt centre you eliminate the outer bias edges, so your quilt centre won't stretch and go wavy.

13 Sew one border strip to the top of your quilt centre and the other to the bottom of your quilt centre. This completes the quilt top.

Quilting and finishing

14 Make a quilt sandwich of the quilt top, the wadding (batting) and the backing fabric (see General Techniques, Making a quilt sandwich).

15 Quilt as desired. My quilt was quilted with a stipple pattern in the background and figure-of-eight style of chain through the fireworks (see General Techniques, Quilting).

16 Square-up and bind to finish (see General Techniques, Squaring-up your quilt and Binding).

Enjoy your quilt.

SHOT IN THE DARK

Designed for scrappy strip lovers who are eco-friendly. Eight large arrows shoot across the top with small arrows, cleverly made from the scraps, filling in the gaps.

Approximate size: 62 x 49in (158 x 125cm)

MATERIALS

- Background – enough grey and black made crumb fabric to cut the pieces listed in Cutting instructions (see Creating the Basics, Making crumb fabric)
- Enough scrappy prints to cut the pieces listed in Cutting instructions
- 70 x 57in (178 x 145cm) of backing fabric
- ⅝yd (60cm) of binding fabric
- 70 x 57in (178 x 145cm) of wadding (batting)

Cutting instructions

Crumb fabric

- Two 7 x 9½in rectangles
- Two 5½ x 62½in rectangles
- Eight 5in squares
- Two 4 x 15½in rectangles
- Sixteen 4 x 8¼in rectangles
- Eight 4in squares
- Four 3 x 5½in rectangles
- Four 3 x 4in rectangles
- Eight 3in squares
- Six 2½ x 22½in rectangles
- One 2½ x 9½in rectangle
- Six 2½ x 4in rectangles
- Sixteen 2 x 9¼in rectangles
- Two 2 x 6½in rectangles
- Four 2 x 6in rectangles
- Four 1½ x 9in strips (you may prefer to cut these narrow pieces from black/grey scraps rather than crumb fabric)

Scrappy prints

- Eight 2 x 17in rectangles
- Sixteen 1¼ x 3¼in strips and strings
- Forty 1–1½in wide x 20in long strips and strings

Binding fabric

- Seven 2½in wide strips across the width of the fabric

Arrow pieces

1 Sew five 20in long strips into a strip set that measures 4¾–5¼ x 20in (see Creating the Basics, Making a strip/string set).

2 Make a 45-degree cut from the bottom left-hand corner to the top edge. Make a parallel 45-degree cut 2½in from the first cut. On the top edge, leave a ¼in space and then make a 45-degree cut from the top edge to bottom edge in the opposite direction. Make a parallel 45-degree cut 2½in from the previous cut. At the right-hand edge, make a vertical (90-degree) cut from the bottom right of the last cut to the top edge of the strip set.

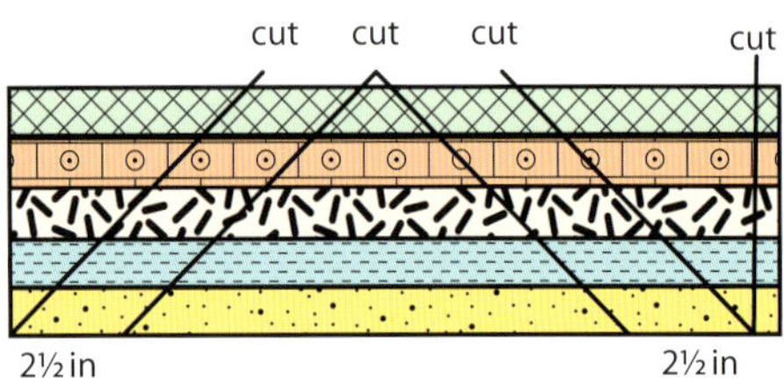

3 Keep the pieces cut in Step 2 organised as shown – the right-hand slither of strip set is not needed. You could put sticky labels on the pieces to help you keep track of what's what.

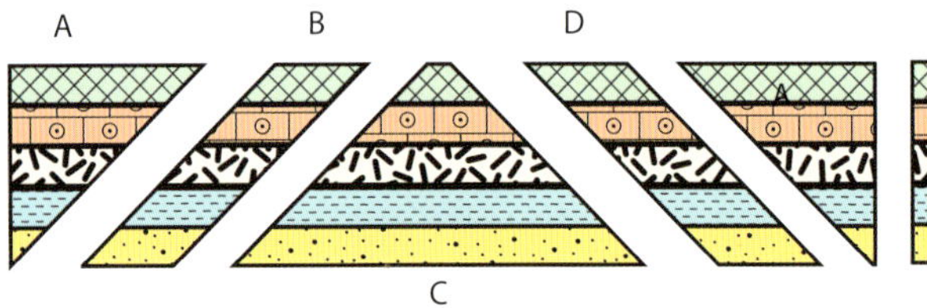

4 Repeat Steps 1–3 seven more times to make a total of eight sets of arrow pieces.

KISS: As the arrows are constructed, units may need trimming or extending depending on the finished width of your starting strip set, so don't panic if you need to tweak things as you go in this freeform style of piecing.

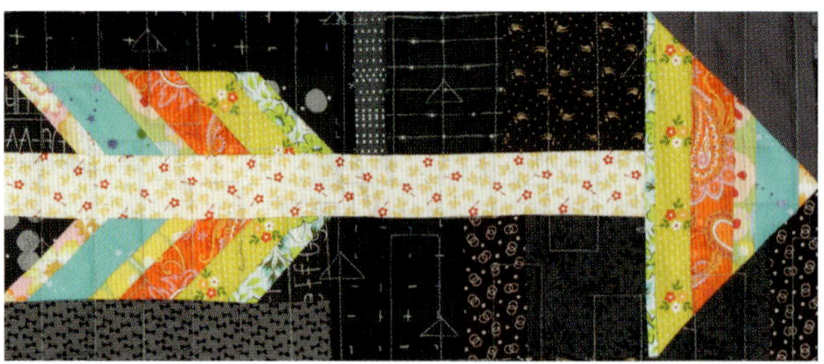

Large arrow blocks

5 Take two 3in crumb squares and cut each once on the diagonal.

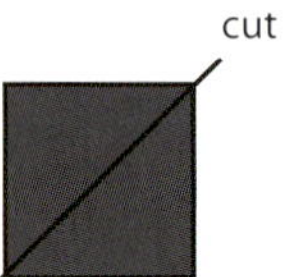

6 Using the same set of arrow pieces, sew the triangles cut in Step 5 to each end of pieces B and D.

7 Sew a 2 x 9¼in crumb rectangle to one long side of B and one long side of D as shown.

8 Sew a 4 x 8¼in crumb rectangle to the top short edge of B and the top short edge of D as shown.

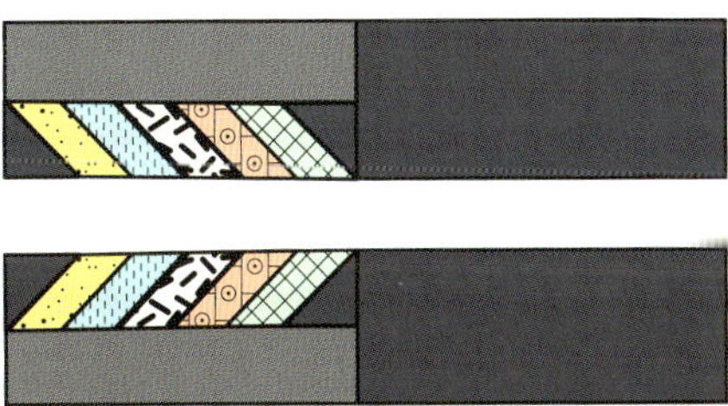

9 Take a 2 x 17in scrappy rectangle. This rectangle will go between the B and D units made in Step 8. Sew the rectangle to the inner long edge of one unit, matching up the short row edges at the bottom of the arrow's fletching (feather-like end). Repeat with the inner long edge of the other unit. If the rectangle extends beyond the top edges of the B and D units, trim so it is level. This completes the fletching and shaft unit. Set aside.

10 Take a 5in crumb square and cut it once on the diagonal to give two triangles. Take piece C from the same set of arrow pieces as B and D. Sew the triangles to either side of C as shown to make a flying goose unit.

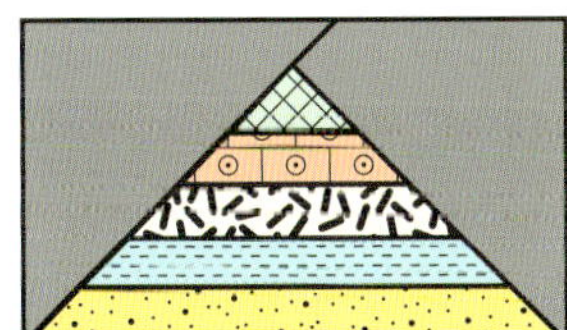

11 The flying goose unit needs to be 9in wide. If the unit is not wide enough, add equal width strips to each side (so the goose tip remains centred). If the unit is too wide, trim equal width strips to each side (so the goose tip remains centred).

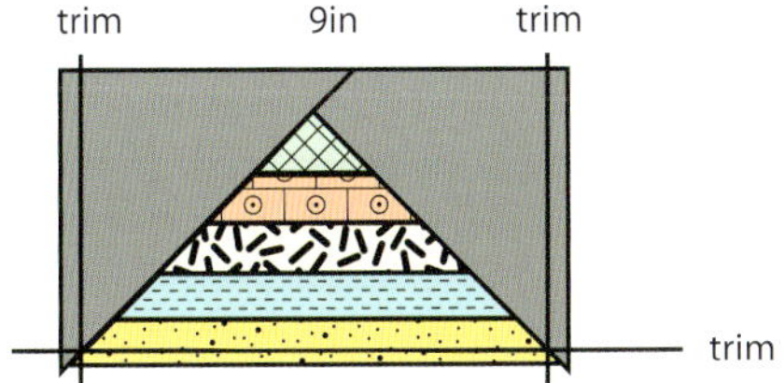

12 Sew the flying goose unit to the top of the fletching and shaft unit made in Step 9.

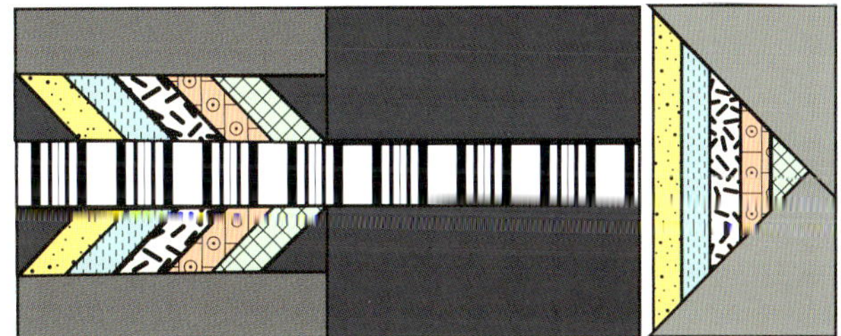

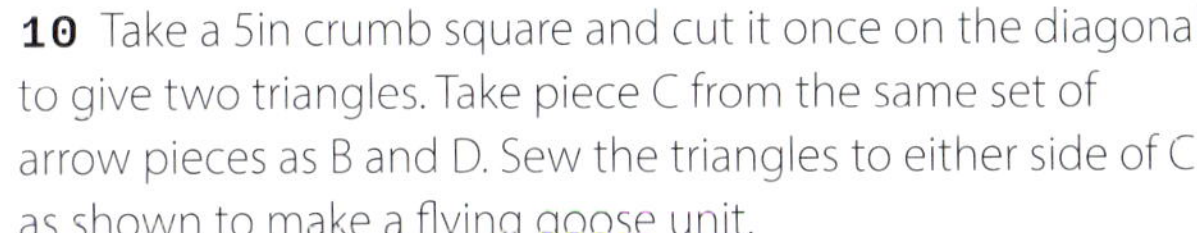

13 The large arrow unit needs to measure 9 x 22½in. If the unit is not quite long enough, add a strip of the required width to the bottom of the unit (the fletching end). This completes one large arrow block.

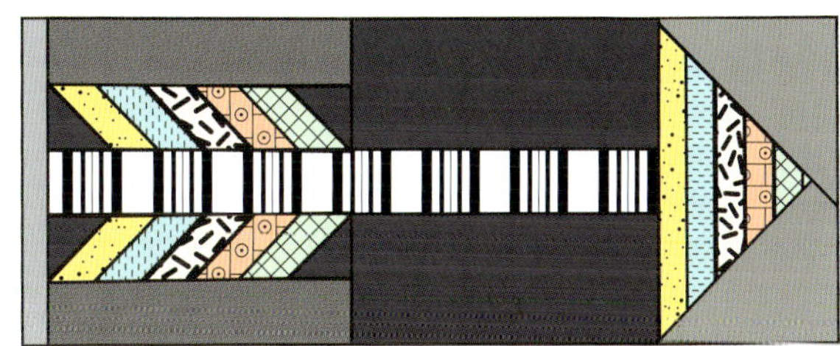

14 Repeat Steps 5–13 to make a total of eight large arrow blocks.

Small arrowheads

15 Take eight 4in crumb squares and cut each once on the diagonal to give sixteen triangles.

16 Take one of the triangles and cut it in half on the diagonal as shown.

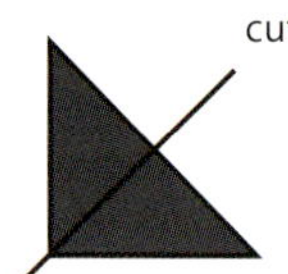

17 Insert a 1¼ x 3¼in scrappy strip between the cut edges, matching up the edges on the diagonal edge as shown.

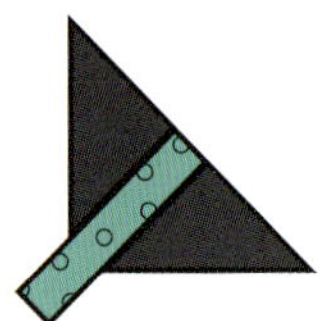

18 Sew the unit made in Step 17 to a piece A on the diagonal edges.

19 Keeping the 45-degree line of your ruler aligned with the central (long) diagonal seam, trim to 4in square. This completes a small arrowhead.

20 Repeat Steps 16–19 to make a total of sixteen small arrowheads.

Small arrow block 1

21 Take two small arrowheads and one 4 x 15½in crumb rectangle. Sew an arrowhead to each short end of the rectangle as shown.

22 Repeat Step 21 to make a second small arrow block 1.

Small arrow block 2

23 Take four small arrowheads, two 2½ x 4in crumb rectangles and one 2½ x 9½in crumb rectangle.

24 Arrange the units as shown. Sew a 2½ x 4in crumb rectangle between two small arrowheads. Repeat. Then sew the 2½ x 9½in crumb rectangle between these units.

25 Take the two 7 x 9½in crumb rectangles and sew one rectangle to two opposite sides of the unit made in Step 24.

Small arrow block 3

26 Take two small arrowheads, two 3 x 4in crumb rectangles and one 2 x 6½in crumb rectangle.

27 Arrange the units as shown. Sew a 3 x 4in crumb rectangle to the bottom of the left-hand arrowhead and sew a 3 x 4in crumb rectangle to the top of the right-hand arrowhead. Then sew the 2 x 6½in crumb rectangle between these units.

28 Repeat Steps 26 and 27 to make a second small arrow block 3.

Small arrow block 4

29 Take one small arrowhead, one 2½ x 4in crumb rectangle, one 2 x 6in crumb rectangle and one 3 x 5½in crumb rectangle.

30 Arrange the units as shown. Sew the 2½ x 4in crumb rectangle to the right-hand side of the arrowhead, the 2 x 6in crumb rectangle to the top and the 3 x 5½in crumb rectangle to the left-hand side.

31 Repeat Steps 29 and 30 to make a total of four small arrow block 4.

Quilt assembly

Follow the layout diagram when constructing the quilt top.

32 For the outer vertical rows, working from top to bottom, join the following units:

- small arrow block 4, with the tip pointing to the top left corner
- large arrow block, with the arrow pointing downwards
- 1½ x 9in crumb strip
- small arrow block 3
- 1½ x 9in crumb strip
- large arrow block, with the arrow pointing upwards
- small arrow block 4, with the tip pointing to the bottom left corner

33 For the centre vertical row, working from top to bottom, join the following units:

- large arrow block, with the arrow pointing left
- 2½ x 22½in crumb-fabric rectangle
- small arrow block 1
- 2½ x 22½in crumb-fabric rectangle
- large arrow block, with the arrow pointing right
- 2½ x 22½in crumb-fabric rectangle
- small arrow block 2
- 2½ x 22½in crumb-fabric rectangle
- large arrow block, with the arrow pointing left
- 2½ x 22½in crumb-fabric rectangle
- small arrow block 1
- 2½ x 22½in crumb-fabric rectangle
- large arrow block, with the arrow pointing right

34 Sew a 5½ x 62½in crumb-fabric rectangle to each long edge of the centre vertical row and then sew an outer vertical row to each side of the quilt centre, noting that you need to turn the row on the right-hand side by 180 degrees so the small arrow block 4 at each end points outwards. This completes your quilt top.

Quilting and finishing

35 Make a quilt sandwich of the quilt top, the wadding (batting) and the backing fabric (see General Techniques, Making a quilt sandwich).

36 Quilt as desired. My quilt was quilted with vertical lines with arrowhead patterns thrown in at random intervals (see General Techniques, Quilting).

37 Square-up and bind to finish (see General Techniques, Squaring-up your quilt and Binding).

Enjoy your quilt.

GENERAL TECHNIQUES

While scrap quilting with strips and crumbs is unique and creates rich and colourful results, adhering to basic quilting guidelines, from cutting to binding, will ensure success in producing a quilt you will be proud to share.

PIECING

Piecing not only creates the look and design of your quilt, but it is also a quilt's underlying structure. Using good piecing techniques will ensure you have a beautiful quilt that will last.

Accurate ¼in seams

In quilt-making, a ¼in seam is used when sewing fabric pieces together. Test your ¼in seam by placing two 2¼ x 4in rectangles right sides together and then sew along one 4in edge. Press the seam to one side. Your piece should measure exactly 4in square. If it doesn't, adjust your needle's position or use a line of masking (painter's) tape on your throat plate, adjusting things until you make a 4in square. Doing this will save you a lot of headaches later. Even very slight variations add up as your quilt grows, making it increasingly difficult to fit things together as the quilt progresses.

Stitch length

I like to use a stitch length that gives approximately twelve stitches per inch. On my sewing machine, this is a setting of 2.5, but it will vary from machine to machine, so your setting may be different, so test a few settings before you begin piecing. If your seams come undone at the ends, try a shorter stitch length. If the seam puckers, or the thread looks too loose, before messing with your machine's tension, there are a few things you can try first: change the needle – a nick or flaw in a needle will affect the way it sews; take out the bobbin and make sure there are no threads or lint messing things up; re-thread your machine – I'm amazed how many times this has fixed my problem; make sure you are using high-quality thread, as this too can affect the running of a machine.

Pinning

A pin can be your best friend, helping you to line up seams and points, and to distribute fabric evenly over longer seams. When 'nesting' seams, pin the side of the seam that will reach the needle last, as this allows you to take out the pin as you are sewing without the seam shifting. When joining sections of your quilt where multiple seams will intersect, use a pin at each intersection. But don't worry too much if not everything matches up perfectly. Quilting is meant to be fun and once the quilt is complete the beauty will shine through and few mismatched seams will only add to the character of your quilt. And most of the time, you'll be the only one that notices anyway.

Chain piecing

Chain piecing is like a mini-assembly line, and is a good way to save time and thread. Once pieces are ready to sew together, you can feed them through your machine one after the other without cutting the thread. Once all the pieces have been sewn, simply clip threads between each unit.

KISS: Before you start chain piecing, make sure your bobbin is full. If it runs out part way through your chain, the chain will fall apart and you will have to go back and re-sew. I've done this far too many times and don't recommend it!

Pressing seams

Generally, seams are pressed towards the darker fabric, but as made crumb fabric contains lots of seams, I prefer to press my seams to the side with the least resistance. Pressing uses the weight of the iron and steam to get your seam to lie flat and remove wrinkles. I like to set the seam first, which just means pressing the seam before the fabric pieces are opened out. Next, I open up the two pieces and press the seam to the path of least resistance. Once again, I place the iron down and press – don't move the iron from side to side as this can cause distortion. I like to use steam. When a piece of made crumb fabric is finished, or I've completed a block, I like to give it a spray with starch and press once more.

I know many quilters press seams open, but I feel this weakens the seam and reduces the durability of the quilt. So I only press a seam open if bulk pressing to either side is an issue.

On-point settings

When setting a quilt on-point the rows are sewn together diagonally instead of in straight horizontal rows. Setting triangles are used to make the edges straight, and corner triangles are added at each corner. If sashing is being used, it is added just as you would with a square-set quilt, but the sashing strips are sewn as part of the diagonal rows.

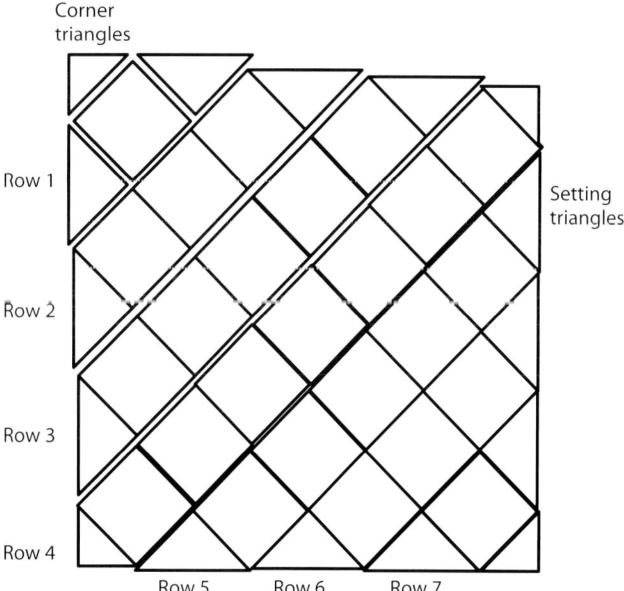

MAKING A QUILT SANDWICH

Making a quilt sandwich, also known as layering or basting, holds the three layers (quilt top, wadding (batting) and backing) of your quilt together to prevent things shifting while you quilt.

There are several basting methods, but I prefer to pin using curved safety pins for quilters. This method is best for machine quilting as it's easy to remove the pins as you work. Quilts can be hand-tacked, but I don't recommend this if you are planning to quilt by machine as the machine's foot can get caught in the tacking stitches. Smaller projects can be spray basted, but this is less successful for larger projects as it's difficult to keep the backing pucker free.

KISS: For larger quilts, the backing and wadding (batting) should be approximately 4in bigger all around than the quilt top. For smaller makes, like runners and pillows, 2in bigger all around is fine.

1 Gather your quilt top, wadding (batting), backing, curved safety pins and masking (painter's) tape. Press your quilt top and backing.

2 Place your backing wrong side up on a large, clean, flat surface. I like to put two banquet tables together, but the floor is fine. Smooth out your backing so it is completely flat and without wrinkles, but don't stretch it. Use masking (painter's) tape to hold it in place on whatever surface you are using. Sometimes, I use large binder clips to hold my layers to the banquet tables, folding the edge of the backing over the lip of the table and using the binder clips to hold it in place.

3 Spread the wadding (batting) on top of the backing. Gently smooth it out from the centre outwards, being careful not to stretch it.

4 Next, right side up, place your quilt top centrally on top of the wadding (batting). Again, smooth out the wrinkles from the centre out, taking care not to stretch or distort it.

5 Using curved safety pins, pin all three layers together in a grid format. Place the pins 4–5in apart all over the quilt's surface.

6 Remove the tape or binder clips and the quilt is ready for quilting.

QUILTING

The quilts in this book were all machine quilted. The smaller ones I did on my domestic machine. My friend, Ruth Davis, quilted the larger ones on her long-arm machine. Hand-quilting is also an option. If you are worried about quilting, there are others who will do it for you for a fee. I recommend asking to see samples of their work, as this will ensure you like their style and helps to eliminate surprises when you get your quilt back.

If you plan to quilt on your domestic machine, I suggest you sketch out a few plans first. This will give you an idea of how a design will look, and it creates 'muscle memory' for when you begin to quilt your quilt for real. I like to take a picture of a section of my quilt and then blow it up in size. I then place clear vinyl or thick plastic over the image and use a dry-erase marker to draw different quilting motifs until I hit on one I like.

When quilting on a domestic machine, it's a good idea to have a table behind you and to the left of your machine, as this will help to support your quilt and take some of the weight, making it easier to move the quilt around as you are quilting. I like to start in the centre of my quilt and work my way outwards. This helps to prevent puckers in the middle of the quilt – and it gets the hardest part to quilt out of the way first. As you get closer to the edges of your quilt, there is less fabric bunched up against your machine, so it's easier to manoeuvre your quilt.

Quilting design options

Choosing a quilt design can be overwhelming. The following suggestions should help to get your creative juices flowing – use them as a starting point and then add your own flair.

Straight-line quilting
It is best to use a walking foot for straight-line quilting. Try spacing your lines at different intervals and at different angles to add more interest to your quilt. A Hera marker or masking (painter's) tape can be used to mark your quilting guidelines. I used straight-line quilting on Shot in the Dark.

Free-motion quilting
This method is done by lowering the feed dogs and using the darning foot. You are in control of the design and the stitch length. It takes practice, so don't expect to be an expert straight away, but once you master the technique it opens up endless possibilities in your quilting designs – essentially, it is like drawing with your machine. If you are a beginner, you may wish to test it out on a few spare quilt sandwich squares or a small project before tackling a large quilt. I used free-motion quilting on Bloom and Jacks.

Gentle curving lines

Allowing the quilted lines to ebb and flow will give a softer, more flowing feel. You can use a walking foot with the feed dogs up, or put the feed dogs down and use the darning foot instead. I use the seams of my rows as guidelines so that my lines don't slowly get wider at one end of the quilt, which would result in more quilting on one side compared to the other. The quilting in Spring Fling is an example of this style.

Highlight the piecing

With this method of quilting, different motifs are placed in the quilting blocks and pieces to set them off. Parella Glam is an example of this kind of quilting.

Overall design

This is where the same design is stitched over the entire quilt surface to showcase the quilt as a whole, rather than highlight individual elements. Streak of Lightning and Escape are examples of this style of quilting.

Fit the theme

Here, the theme or inspiration for the quilt is taken through into the quilting. Rainbow Star and Fireworks are examples of this style of quilting.

SQUARING-UP YOUR QUILT

This step is in preparation for binding your quilt. Start by placing a 6 x 24in ruler in one corner of your quilt, so that the 6in side is along the bottom edge and the 24in side runs up the side edge.

Straighten and adjust your quilt top edge so that it lines up along your ruler and you have a 90-degree angle at the corner. Trim the excess backing and wadding (batting). Continue around the edge of your quilt creating straight edges and 90-degree angles at the corners.

BINDING

The binding gives a finished edge to your quilted quilt. It is like a frame and is the last design choice you will make on your quilt. Audition different bindings by placing fabric along the quilt's edge so that only ¼in is showing. This will give you a feel for what your binding will look like on your quilt.

Binding can be cut on the straight grain of your fabric or on the bias (at a 45-degree angle). A straight-grain binding is faster and requires less fabric. A bias-cut binding will wear better. Whatever your chosen method, cut enough 2½in wide strips so that when joined with 45-degree seams the long strip will go all around your quilt plus 8–10in.

1 Right sides together, sew your binding strips into one long length using 45-degree seams. Press the seams open to reduce bulk and trim the 'ears'.

2 Fold the strip in half lengthwise, wrong sides together, and press.

3 Working from the right side and starting part way down one edge – I usually start on the bottom edge – match the raw edges of the binding to the raw edges of the quilt, leaving an 8–10in tail.

4 Sew in place. When you come to a corner, pull your binding back so it lines up with the next edge of your quilt. Finger-press and carefully bring the end of the binding back so it lines up with the next edge of your quilt. Pin the resulting pleat at the corner. Then start sewing down the next edge. This is called a mitred corner.

5 When you get about 15in from where you began sewing your binding, stop. Line up your two binding ends along the edge of your quilt, folding back where they meet and creating a ½in gap between them. From each fold, measure back 1⅛in and cut the end of your binding. Take left side of the binding and line up the edge that is next to the quilt to right side of the binding that is away from the quilt – the short side of each will run down the long side of the other. Pin and sew a 45-degree seam. Trim the seam allowance and continue to sew the binding in place.

6 Fold the binding over to the back of the quilt and neatly slipstitch the folded edge to the backing fabric by hand.

KISS: When joining the ends of my binding, I always check to make sure everything fits before I trim the seam allowance.

Scrappy binding

Instead of using strips cut across the width of fabric, why not follow the scrappy theme through to your binding? For this method use wider strips, 4½–8in wide.

1 Sew strips together, staggering the beginning of the strips. Do this by making a 45-degree angle fold and lining up the edge of the next strip where the edge lines up. Doing this reduces waste.

2 Continue adding strips in this fashion until the piece is approximately 18in wide.

3 Line up the 45-degree line of your cutting ruler along a long edge of your fabric and cut strip at a 45-degree angle.

4 Line up the edge of your ruler along the previously made cut to start cutting strips for your binding. Sometimes, I like to use a narrower binding, and in this case I cut my binding strips 2¼in wide, so lined up my ruler accordingly. Continue to cut binding strips in this manner.

5 Join the binding strips by placing right sides together with the tips extending ¼in as shown. Then stitch in place.

6 Repeat this process to make the required length of binding.

QUILT LABELS

It is a good idea to add a label to your quilt. It should contain the name of the quilt, who made it, where they live, the date it was finished and any other information you would like to include.

I find the easiest way for me to add a label is to fold an 8in square of fabric in half along the diagonal. Using a permanent fabric pen, I write the information I wish to include onto one triangle of the folded square. Then I sew the raw edges of the triangle into a corner on the back of the quilt when sewing the binding in place. Then all I have to do is hand slipstitch the folded diagonal edge of the label to the quilt backing.

TEMPLATES

Templates are shown at actual size. Downloadable versions of these templates are available at www.bookmarkedhub.com.

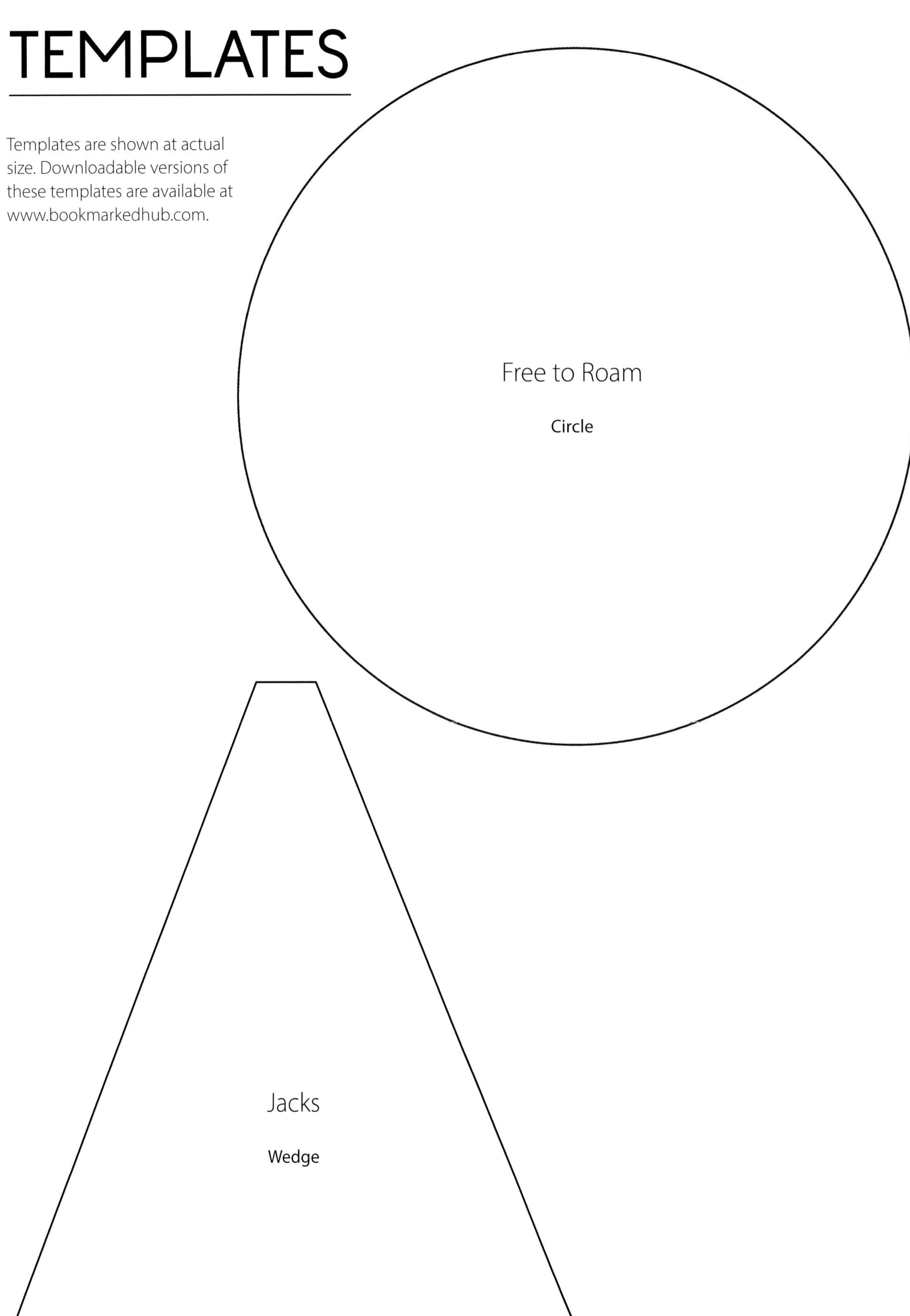

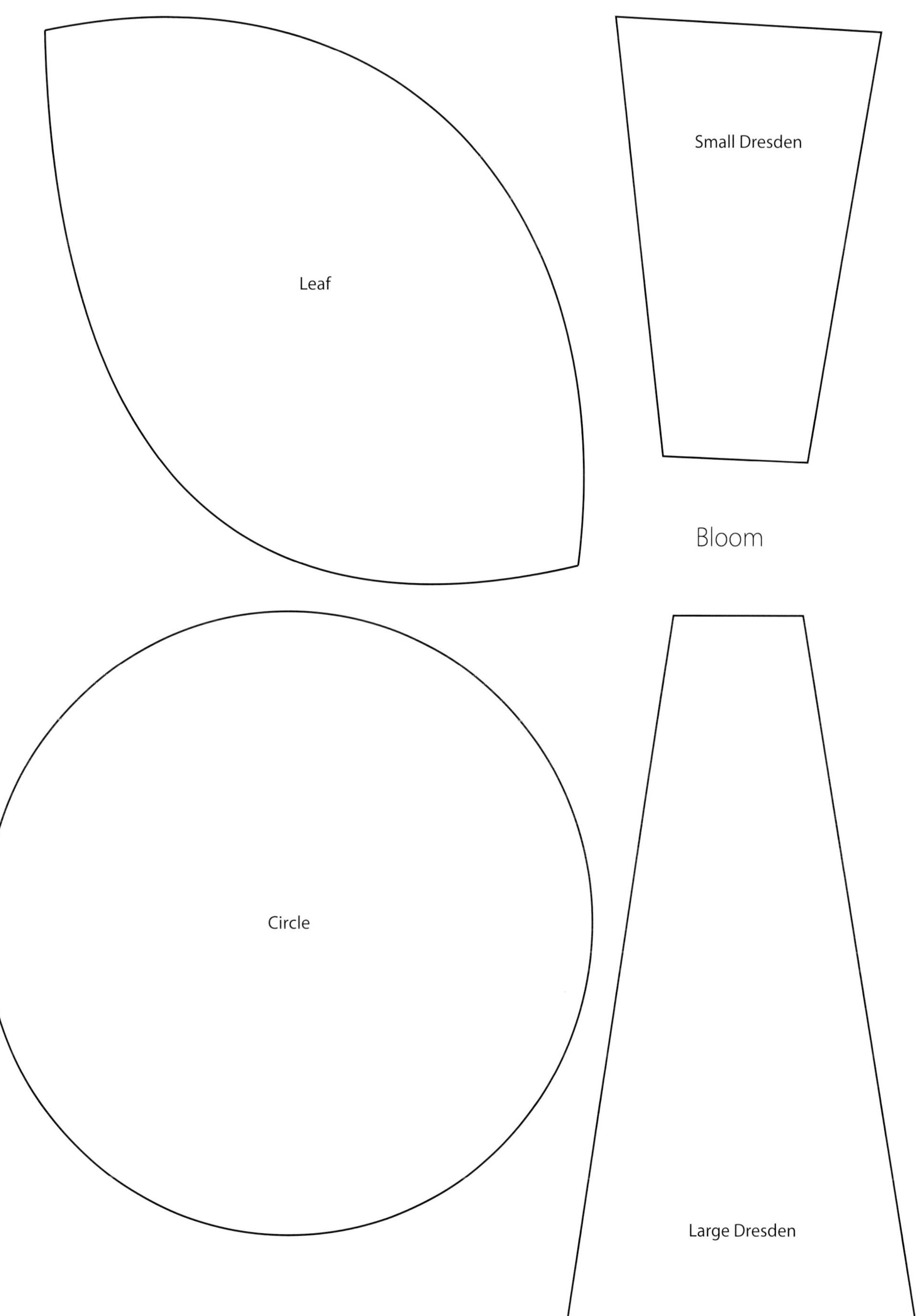
Leaf
Small Dresden
Bloom
Circle
Large Dresden

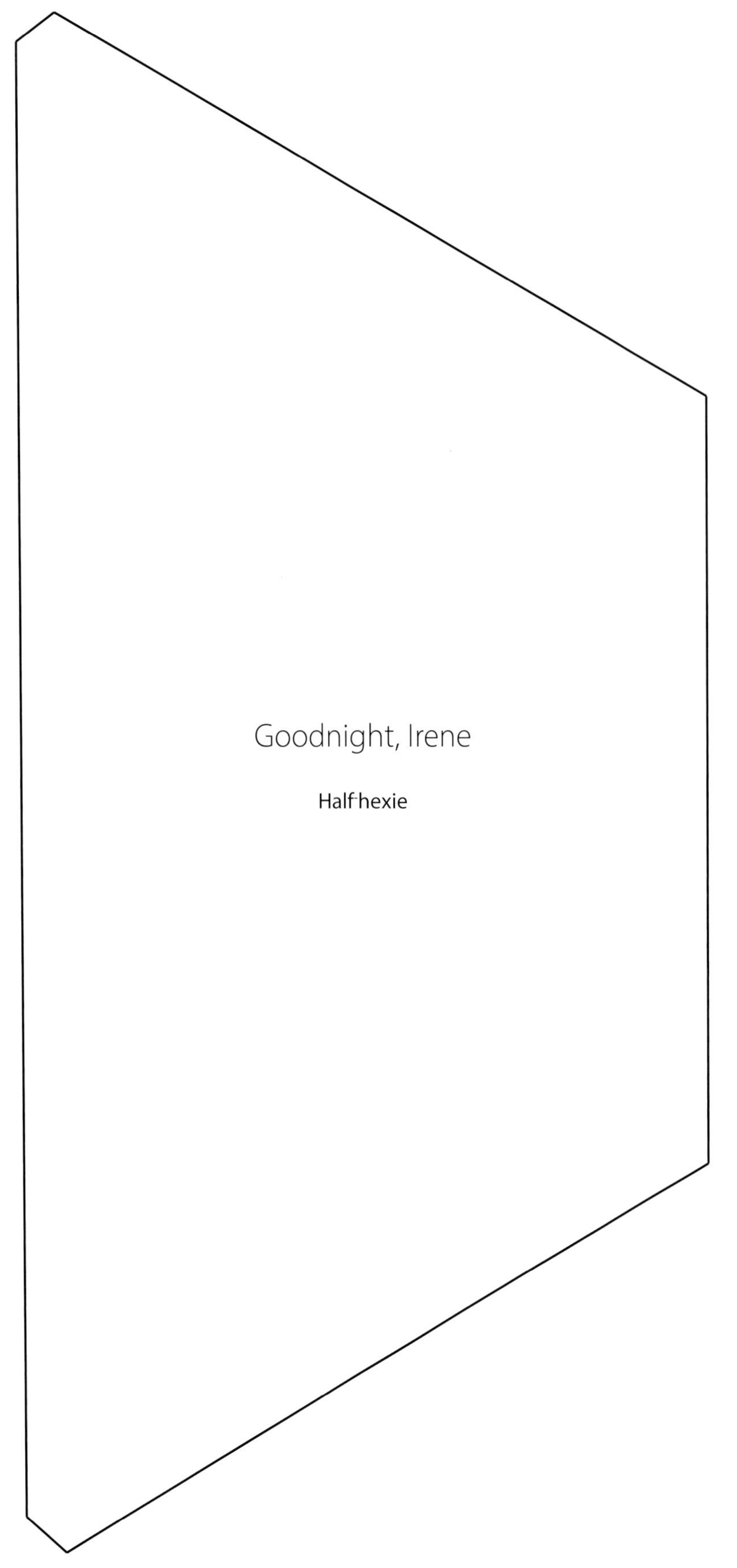
Goodnight, Irene
Half-hexie

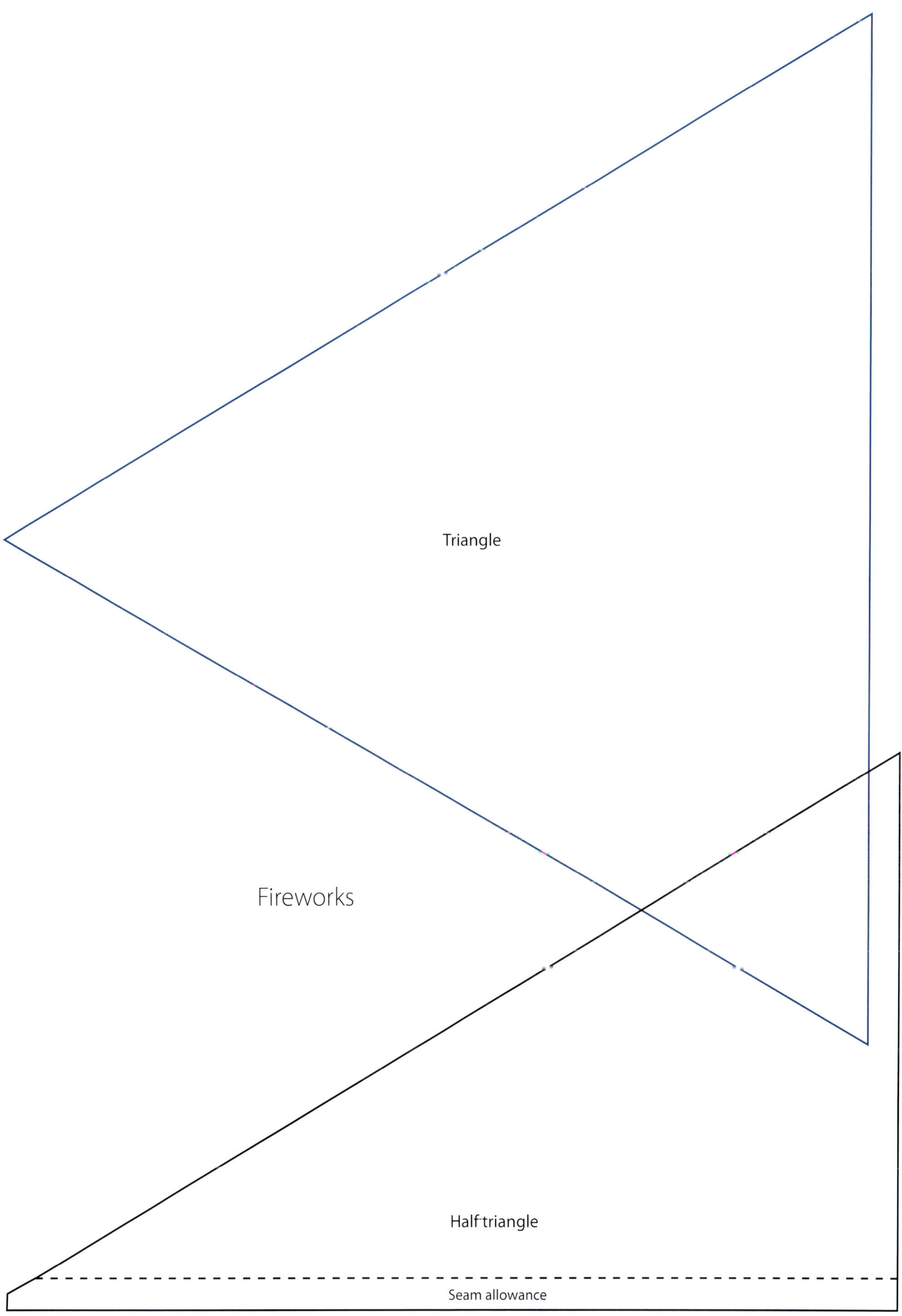
Triangle
Fireworks
Half triangle
Seam allowance

ABOUT THE AUTHOR

Emily Bailey, the creative force behind Aunt Em's Quilts, grew up in a home filled with artistic inspiration. Surrounded by creativity from a young age, she developed a deep appreciation for art and design, which eventually blossomed into a passion for quilting. Emily specialises in scrap quilting, delighting in transforming fabric leftovers into beautiful, meaningful creations.

Driven by her desire to help others discover the joy of creating, Emily shares her knowledge through her quilt patterns, workshops and inspiring projects. She is immensely grateful for the friendships and connections quilting has brought into her life, cherishing the sense of community and camaraderie it fosters. She believes quilters are uniquely generous, with an uncanny ability to pick up the pieces – both literally and figuratively – and turn them into something beautiful. Through her work, she strives to make the world a softer, snugglier place, one quilt at a time. Whether you're a seasoned quilter or just beginning your journey, Emily's heartfelt designs are sure to inspire your creativity and love for quilting, too.

www.auntemsquilts.com

ACKNOWLEDGEMENTS

Thank you to: Tim, the love of my life – he is the string to my kite, my stabilising force; my mom, whose encouragement keeps me going when things get hard; my dad, who built my workstation so I have a lovely place to create; my children, Alex, Joshua, Neil and Anna, for their friendship and support; and my dear friend and partner in crime, Ruth Davis – her gift for long-arm quilting takes my creations to a new level. Thanks, too, to Sarah Callard for allowing me this opportunity to share my love of quilting, and to Anne Williams for taking my creative spelling and grammar and making it coherent. And a special thanks to all the wonderful staff at David & Charles, who know how to make a beautiful book.

INDEX

A DAVID AND CHARLES BOOK

David and Charles is an imprint of David and Charles, Ltd
Suite A, Tourism House, Pynes Hill, Exeter, EX2 5WS

First published in the UK and USA in 2025

A catalogue record for this book is available from the British Library.

ISBN-13: 9781446315262 paperback
ISBN-13: 9781446315286 EPUB

This book has been printed on paper from approved suppliers and made from pulp from sustainable sources.

Printed in China through Asia Pacific Offset for:
David and Charles, Ltd
Suite A, Tourism House, Pynes Hill, Exeter, EX2 5WS

10 9 8 7 6 5 4 3 2 1

Publishing Director: Ame Verso
Senior Commissioning Editor: Sarah Callard
Publishing Manager: Jeni Chown
Editor: Victoria Allen
Project Editor: Anne Williams
Lead Designer: Sam Staddon
Designer: Lucy Ridley
Pre-press Designer: Susan Reansbury
Design and Art Direction: Sarah Rowntree
Photography: Jason Jenkins
Production Manager: Beverley Richardson

Full-size printable versions of the templates are available to download free from www.bookmarkedhub.com. Search for this book by the title or ISBN: the files can be found under 'Book Extras'. Membership of the Bookmarked online community is free.

The publisher would like to thank Rafikis (rafikis.co.uk) for allowing us to shoot at their cafe-bar-restaurant. We would also like to thank Heron Valley (heronvalley.co.uk) for allowing us to shoot at their bar and coffee shop. Thank you also to Quilt Direct for allowing us to use their AccuQuilt machine for the photograph in Tools & Materials.